Ten Foolish Dating Mistakes That Men
And Women Make
(And How To Avoid Them)

TEN FOOLISH DATING MISTAKES THAT MEN AND WOMEN MAKE
(AND HOW TO AVOID THEM)

by
Lila Gruzen, Ph.D., M.F.C.C.
Rebecca Sperber, M.S., M.F.C.C.

Griffin Publishing Group
Glendale, California

Publisher: Robert Howland
Director of Operations: Robin Howland
Managing Editor: Marjorie L. Marks
Book Design: Mark M. Dodge
Cover Design: Big Fish
Contributing Editor: Janet Eastman

10 9 8 7 6 5 4 3 2 1

ISBN 1-882180-87-9

Griffin Publishing Group
544 Colorado Street
Glendale, California 91204

Telephone: (818) 244-1470

Manufactured in the United States of America

DEDICATION 1

I DEDICATE THIS BOOK TO MY DAD, JACK GRUZEN, WHO ALWAYS BELIEVED THAT I COULD ACCOMPLISH ANYTHING, AND TO MY MOM, GUTA GRUZEN, WHO DID ALL THE WORRYING, SAVING ME A GREAT DEAL OF TIME AND ENERGY. I FURTHER DEDICATE THIS BOOK TO THE BEST DATE I'VE EVER HAD, MY BOYFRIEND AND WONDERFUL HUSBAND, BRIAN LINK. I THANK MY SONS, GRIFFIN AND CONNOR, FOR MAKING ME SMILE IN A PART OF MY SOUL THAT PREVIOUSLY WAS UNKNOWN. FINALLY, A HUGE THANK YOU TO MY FAMILY AND FRIENDS WHO HELD MY HAND AND HELPED ME RETAIN MY SANITY THROUGH ALL THOSE YEARS OF DATING. YOU KNOW WHO YOU ARE!

—L.G.

DEDICATION 2

I DEDICATE THIS BOOK TO MY MOM, EDIE SPERBER, MY DAD, EDDIE SPERBER, AND BROTHERS, SCOTT AND JACK SPERBER, FOR THEIR LOVE AND SUPPORT AND FOR ALWAYS ENCOURAGING ME TO WRITE. TO MY HUSBAND, MICHAEL COMPEAN, AND MY LITTLE BOYS, ADAM AND BEN, FOR UNDERSTANDING WHEN I HAD TO WRITE INSTEAD OF PLAY. AND TO ALL THE MEN I'VE DATED WHO'VE TAUGHT ME ABOUT THE NEGATIVE AND POSITIVE ASPECTS OF RELATIONSHIPS, AND WHO HELPED INSPIRE ME TO WRITE THIS BOOK.

—R.S.

CONTENTS

Introduction

The mistakes explored in this book are "foolish" because they destroy any chance of finding a lasting relationship. These mistakes in behavior and attitude may have become rigid parts of your "dating persona" that push intimacy away.

This book is about developing personal rules of behavior and attitude that create healthy, positive, romantic relationships. The goal of other popular books about dating rules (men's rules, women's rules, the right rules, the wrong rules) is to present you with a formula of behavior that will help snag a partner. "Do this or do that and love will follow" is a common theme. But the "this or that" usually involves trying to figure out some way to control or outwit the opposite sex based on a set of beliefs that pit men and women against each other.

We believe that focusing on the differences between men and women distracts people from the real problem, which is the need *to face your own faulty attitudes and behaviors.* Both men and women sabotage relationships by committing similar types of "dating mistakes," including being too picky, communicating poorly, or getting involved too quickly, to name only a few. We want to show both men and women how to stop ruining their chances for lasting love.

Whose Fault Is It, Anyway?

If you are taking the time to read this book, you are probably frustrated and worried about the fact that your relationships keep failing. You are not alone. People are struggling with this issue in epidemic proportion. As many among the frustrated put it, *"I want to meet someone and settle down, but either I can't find someone who feels 'right' or I keep getting dumped."* The reason the solution to the problem eludes so many single people is that they blame others rather than looking at their own behavior.

The concept, *"If you're still single it's your fault,"* is what this book is all about. This is not to imply that you are bad, unintelligent, or emotionally disturbed. All people struggle with negative attitudes and behaviors that develop over the years as a result of life experiences and influences. What we are saying is: If you continue to be disappointed in the outcome of your dating relationships, then *discovering your own contribution to past disasters increases your future chances of creating the outcome you desire.*

Our objective is that this be the last book you need to buy to help you find a lasting relationship.

We acknowledge that in some ways men and women *are* stereotypically different from each other. We also contend, however, that men and women are more *alike* than different concerning their needs and wants in relationships. We believe that all of you who are reading this book are good people who may be making some bad mistakes. But it's time to face the fact that when bad results continue to recur in your dating relationships, *you* are partly to blame. Such behaviors are not intentional but, rather, are *learned* defensive behaviors that are designed to protect you from further hurt.

WHERE DID WE LEARN SUCH BEHAVIORS?

These "foolish mistakes" were taught to you by others, primarily through behavior modeled by family members or other authority figures. You may have left home with ingrained maladaptive ways of behaving. Many of us enter adulthood without having learned to express our feelings effectively, to argue constructively, or to love fully. We then start dating and turn into the Saturday night "date from hell" for some other innocent person.

IS IT TOO LATE FOR ME?

The good news is that *learned behavior can be unlearned.* This is the major goal of *Ten Foolish Dating Mistakes*—to show you how to stop making those mistakes and develop behavior that is conducive to lasting love and romance.

We know that you may have been dumped, hurt and disappointed by relationships. It is difficult to be trusting and optimistic after such bad experiences. It becomes easy to forget that relationships can be fun, safe, and exciting. We are here to remind you that they can be. Our book is going to show you how to become the kind of partner you would like to have for yourself. We will also show you how to spot a dating lemon and how to leave a bad relationship.

In the process, we will share our years of personal and professional experience with relationships, including *why they fail and how they succeed.* We were once in the singles trenches too, and we know how hard and disillusioning being single can be if your goal is to be in a committed relationship. We offer you hope. We found wonderful relationships by practicing the simple principle of focusing on our own attitudes and behaviors—and by learning to *stop placing blame on others.* We learn nothing about ourselves if the focus remains on how *they* blew it, rather than how *we* contributed to the problem.

You don't have to continue to be lonely. In fact, if you want a romantic relationship you should be able to have one! (You don't really prefer 5,000-piece jigsaw puzzles over a relationship, do you?)

We believe that you deserve to have what you desire in a relationship. We are excited about the road map we are providing for you here. When you finish the last page of this book, we know that you will be ready for love—not the "foolish" type but, rather, the kind that can grow, last, and satisfy....

CHAPTER ONE

Foolish Dating Mistake # 1

YOU GIVE TOO MUCH TOO SOON

QUIZ:

You are too hasty with your generosity if any of the following sounds familiar:

1. Your ears ring for weeks as a result of listening to someone's recounting of every second of the last movie they saw.

2. You tell your date about every sexual experience you have ever had and then perform them all that night.

3. After the first date you invite your new friend's family to live with you.

These actions may temporarily make you the most popular single in town, but also will eventually lead to your dating demise.

It is difficult to tell the difference between being generous and giving too much too soon. Yet, the ability to tell the difference between the two can be the deciding factor in either saving or ruining your relationships. To make the distinction, giving too much too soon says, "I am desperate for you to like me." On the other hand, being generous says, "I like you and would enjoy giving this to you."

Even if you are in a current relationship and have already been giving too much too soon, it's not too late to slow things down.

WHY WE GIVE TOO MUCH TOO SOON

Giving too much too soon is a common and easy mistake to make. It is a tempting error because it feels good to give to others. Giving makes us feel involved and intimate. It also can distract us from being aware of our own issues, needs and desires. We do this because it is sometimes uncomfortable and hard work to notice and deal with our own lives. So we focus on the lives of others.

It is a good idea to put some thought into having the amount you give remain in balance with the amount of time you have known the person you're dating. The most common ways of giving too much too soon are:

1. gifts
2. information and secrets
3. being overly empathetic and co-dependent
4. sex
5. incorporating him/her into your life

GIFT GIVING TOO SOON

The name of the gift-giving game is to have the kind of gift equal the maturity of the relationship. Giving too much stuff too soon is sometimes the way of covering up our insecurity. If you are worried about your date liking you, it may be tempting to use gifts as a distraction. Showing up with all kinds of bells and whistles may be thought of as a way to get people to look past our faults and like us right away because we are giving them something. It is possible that you do not feel like you are enough and cannot show up for a date without a prop of some sort to direct the initial attention elsewhere. In this situation, the gift would be as if to say, "Don't look at me, look at what I brought for you."

Compliments also are considered gifts and should be given in an appropriate manner. "You look nice" is appropriate for a first date, as opposed to saying, "Those pants really show off your figure." Respecting both the boundaries and sensibilities of your date should be the deciding factor in what compliment to give.

GUIDELINES FOR APPROPRIATE GIFT GIVING

Note: The following Guidelines regarding number of dates are approximate milestones in the stages of relationships. While optimally healthy relationships develop sequentially through each of these stages, the precise number of dates necessary to achieve each stage varies from couple to couple. Our point is to show that there are stages of a relationship that can be approximated by how many times you share time and experience with a person. Being able to communicate just how interested you are in your partner at the appropriate stage can intensify the intimacy and motivate each person in the relationship to feel valued and desired. This becomes fertile ground for the kind of love you are most likely seeking.

EARLY STAGE OF A RELATIONSHIP

1-10 Dates   Gift: A single flower, casual dinner out or chocolates.

Compliment: "You look nice tonight."

MIDDLE STAGE OF A RELATIONSHIP

11-20 Dates   Gift: Mixed bouquet of flowers, full evening at the theater and dinner, gift appropriate to a holiday.

Compliment: "You look great. I really love your hair."

In the middle stage of dating, compliments can be of a more personal nature ("You have such beautiful eyes."). Gifts can be a bit more significant in value. At this stage you probably will have more feelings for the person, and it is appropriate that the gift express this.

LATER STAGE OF A RELATIONSHIP

20 Dates to   Gift: Romantic cards in the mail, roses, cologne
6 Months   or perfume, surprise dates (more extravagant).

Compliment: "Your honesty and ethics/openness to listening to the other side/loyalty to your friends, etc. impresses me." "How great you smell or how well you kiss," etc.

COMMITMENT STAGE OF A RELATIONSHIP

6 Months On   Gift: Jewelry, clothing.

Compliment: "You are so sexy. I really love your lips."

At the later stage of a relationship, gifts and compliments should be a part of deepening the level of intimacy and commitment. If you get this far into a relationship with someone, a healthy level of communication and trust should support flexibility and risk-taking when it comes to giving.

The bottom line regarding gift giving is to be careful not to overwhelm the other person with a Las Vegas extravaganza of gifts. Try not to allow material things to represent who you are. Have some faith that the right person will be interested in what is unique about you. If this sounds hard to do, it may be a good idea to do some self-esteem calisthenics before you go out with someone. Try sitting down and making a list of "Reasons Why I Am Extremely Datable." Include emotional, physical and social attributes on this list. Reread the list until it is your mantra for self-worth. In order to stay positive and put your best foot forward in the initial stage of dating, you must keep your positive qualities in the forefront of your thinking.

HOW TO DEAL WITH THE EXCESSIVE GIFT GIVER

If you become the recipient of excessive giving of gifts, you must be willing to say, "No." Turn them down and speak about the discomfort that you might feel. This is a perfect time in your new relationship to set boundaries that will help slow down the pace. If you don't, the relationship might start off with a bang and stop with a thud before you know what happened.

TOO MUCH INFORMATION TOO SOON

If you are a person who likes to tell your life story within the first few dates, you are giving too much information too soon. Here in the following First Date Chatter is an example of this:

Him/Her: So how do you like this restaurant? I took a chance that you would enjoy Italian food.

You: Yes, I love Italian food. It reminds me of my grandparents who came here from Italy. They were very, very poor and, in fact, my parents both came from poor families and so even though my Dad made a decent living, there was always fighting in my home about money. I used to lie in bed and worry about it as well. I felt that I had to sell lemonade in order to help us keep the house. And when my Mom drank too much, I would vow to one day be on my own and have enough money to be completely independent...

Stop Talking!!

WHY WE TALK & TELL TOO MUCH

If you do anything that even vaguely reminds you of that outpouring of information, please keep reading. There are two major reasons why we allow our mouths to run over. The first is that we are rambling. Very few people are perfectly comfortable in the Initial Phase of dating. On the first date, or first few dates, we often feel like silence is some kind of date death and we attempt to avoid it at all costs. Many people pull up whatever information comes to mind and let it out of their mouths as if they are confiding in a dear friend. Any topic that arises is an opportunity for you to tell another personal story, secret or heavy piece of information to the stranger known as your date.

The other reason people tell too much is because they have no boundaries. Maybe you come from a family where everyone talked to everybody about everything so you think this behavior is normal. Or maybe you come from a family so secretive that you're dying to tell something to anyone at anytime. Without appropriate boundaries, you overwhelm people with the personal nature of your conversation when no personal relationship exists. Remember the general rule: The amount of information should equal the maturity of the relationship.

Then there is the justification for over-sharing that says, "I want to be known for who I am. I want to achieve this through total openness." The truth is, we all want to be known, especially by our intimate partners. But you are not an intimate partner with someone you have just met. Sure, it feels great when someone knows our favorite wine, the movie that makes us cry, what makes us lose our temper and how much money we invest in the weekly Lotto. But be patient. This onslaught of information does not create a history with the person. It is only through sharing information over time that we become known to our partner in an intimate way.

If you find yourself babbling, stop your thought process immediately and ask your date a question to switch the focus from youself to him/her. You can also note something of interest in the restaurant and discuss that. Before the date, make a short list of topics to turn to in case you find yourself about to reveal what you may later regret.

THE DRAWBACK OF TOO MUCH INFORMATION TOO SOON

One negative effect of turning a stranger into instant confidante is that it may cause us to be rejected. For the relationship-deprived person, this is a devastating result from sharing intimate information. Your date may be repelled by the heavy matters that seem out of context compared to the person he or she is getting to know. None of us could adequately represent ourselves within a date or two. Knowing that you were on Prozac for two years can lead to a false assumption, while hearing about it on the fourteenth date (after spending months getting to know you), makes it possible for your date to process the information in a more positive and accurate way.

DIALOGUE EXAMPLE/FIRST DATE

Date: I was on Prozac for two years.

You: Really?
(In your head—Wow! He/She must have been depressed and suicidal. Maybe he/she is a loser who needs drugs just to go to work.)

DIALOGUE EXAMPLE/FOURTEENTH DATE

Date: Since we are watching this program on antidepressants, I would like to share that I took them for two years.

You: Really? I notice that sometimes you get down, but you seem to know how to make yourself feel better. I'd be interested to hear what you went through that made you depressed.

Date: I took Prozac during a period following my mother's death. Until I took Prozac, I couldn't seem to begin grieving. Then I had three years of great therapy and felt closure. I learned a lot and the experience, though painful, was an important one.

You: Do you worry that the depression will come back?

Date: No, it's been ten years and I seem to be fine. It was just a really tough time then.

The first dialogue illustrates how certain types of personal information can scare someone away because it leads to false assumptions. The second dialogue deals with the same subject matter being discussed by two people who have some history together and some foundation for caring and friendship.

Guidelines For Appropriately Sharing Information

Beginning Stage Of Relationship

1-10 Dates   Keep most important information to yourself, such as strong political beliefs, family trauma, heavy life stories, your long road through drug addiction, etc.

Exceptions are your marital status, number of children and other initially pertinent facts that your date should know.

Middle Stage Of Relationship

11-25 Dates   Share who and/or what plays an important part in your life—for example, "I am close to one of my brothers, because he is always there for me."

Statements revealing why you chose your career, how you feel about certain aspects of your past and present life.

Longer Stage Of Relationship

26 Dates to
6 Months   It is now appropriate to confide in your partner about deeper conflicts and concerns in your life. It's now time to discuss fears, medical issues, strong values, beliefs and life goals. Also, it is appropriate to share important thoughts and feelings about your partner.

At the later stages of the relationship, you are sharing information with someone with whom you have a foundation and a friendship that can bear the weight of heavier matters. If both partners are mature and ready for a relationship, vulnerable sharing can create a trust that deepens the relationship.

What You Should Reveal In The Early Stage

It is fair to reveal certain personal details of your life with a new partner. Even during the beginning stages of a relationship—before any history or trust develops—people deserve to be told certain things. Any aspect of ourselves that could possibly affect our partner in a negative way should be shared, such as:

◊ You must tell someone if you are married or exclusively involved.

◊ You should let them know if you're planning to move far away in the near future.

◊ You must warn your partner if you have a sexually transmittable disease before you have sex with him/her.

Think seriously before deciding to reveal such information. If you feel there is a chance that the relationship may not last, or that the withheld information will in no way impact the other person, it is appropriate to wait to self-disclose. Example:

A 40-year-old woman has herpes. She has had five dates with a man, and is a long way from sexual contact with him. He has expressed no opinion or concerns about sexually transmittable diseases. He has shown no signs of trying to escalate sexual contact.

In this scenario, it is understandable that the woman chose not to disclose that she has this virus. Sexuality has not become a part of their relationship. It is not even being discussed yet.

It is appropriate to protect your privacy in the early stages of a relationship when your personal "secrets" have nothing to do with your new partner and pose no threat. Only as a relationship grows, as the foundation gets stronger, and as you begin to trust the other person, should very personal information be shared. The beginning of a relationship should be about having a good time, to just relax and take things slowly. Deep and meaningful exchanges have to wait. They do not come along like a drive through a fast-food restaurant, but, rather, unfold like a fine dining experience.

BEING OVERLY EMPATHETIC

You are a great person and friend to all—and the ultimate pain sponge. Everyone feels comfortable talking to you, and they all do. Empathy is a wonderful trait, but if you gain your self-esteem by feeling the feelings of others above your own, you are co-dependent. Overly empathetic people give cues to others that it is O.K. to disregard them. These cues may be verbal or nonverbal. They may be obvious or subtle.

Example:

Date: I am so angry at my boss that I could scream.

You: (Pain Sponge, after a hard day at work) Oh, really? Tell me what happened. Start from the beginning and tell me everything.

Date: Explains situation at work.

You: Wow! That's awful! What a jerk your boss is. I can't believe he would act that way. If I were you, I would really let him have it. I could help you write a letter to let him know where you stand.

Date: Really? But I wanted to watch that movie on television.

You: Don't worry. I will write the letter first and if you like it, I will type it up and make a copy at the store.

Date: Well, if you don't mind. You are so nice and understanding. And while you are at the store, could you pick up some munchies?

Because you are willing to lend that extra ear too soon, you put yourself in danger of being used or, at the very least, being the eternal buddy of all whom you date. Healthy romance rarely grows from the buddy system because you have accidentally positioned yourself as even less than a friend. You are the person he or she can always count on to listen, run errands, do the laundry and be there. Your status is closer to "Rover" than to "Lover."

WHY WOULD PEOPLE PUT THEMSELVES IN THIS POSITION?

If you do not believe that you are a find, a quality person who has everything and is going to be an equal partner, then you offer up your services as Mr./Ms. Nice. Again, being nice is great, but when being nice takes precedence over being whom you are, it becomes co-dependency. You are actually saying, "Look at what I can do for you" instead of, "Look at who I am." Such a distorted mission places the focus on your date's life at the expense of your own.

Their needs are considered over your own. Their calendar, schedule, preferences in food, need to sleep, work, their moods and more become the priority in your life. Many co-dependent partners feel as if they have left their life in limbo to tend to the life of the other. It takes vigilance and courage to stick with your own issues. Sometimes it's boring and difficult to follow through on a change we know we need to make in our lives in order to feel better and happier.

If you find that your *main* focus is on the person you are dating, you have taken a trip to this place. The truly dangerous consequence of going there is how right it can feel. It feels safe and warm. You feel trusted and very needed. Your partner seems to be depending increasingly on you and the more of your own life you give up, the more you can attend to his or her life.

And just when you think all is well, the yummy safety rug gets pulled. This person for whom you have given so much, falls for another (who is not nearly as nice as you). When you're struggling to figure out how you could be so easily dismissed, keep in mind that overly empathetic and co-dependent partners are perfect foils for people who don't want to put effort into a real relationship. They get to be totally self-centered and not have to worry about you at all. If you begin to bring up your needs, they will switch to how that affects them. *Remember, you taught them to disregard your needs by not allowing your needs to be considered and met. We teach people, from the very beginning, how to treat us.*

WHERE DOES THIS COME FROM & HOW DO YOU GET OUT OF IT?

Your family members may have been either overly involved, enmeshed in each other's lives or cold and detached. Enmeshed relationships operate by the rule: "Your problems, your feelings and your situations also are mine." This may have taught you to immediately take on the lives and feelings of those people in your life, no matter how casual those relationships might be. This may feel normal for you. Initially, people will love you for this. No one can cook up a meal, lend a large sum of money and listen nonstop to every problem while smiling and looking like a million bucks better than you!

If your family was cold and detached, you may feel like a heat-seeking missile in search of closeness at any cost. You may believe that there is a huge cost in obtaining love if it wasn't given freely in your childhood.

Example of being vacant (The message is: "Don't worry about me."):

Date: Would you like to go to dinner?

You: (who haven't yet eaten) No. You don't need to spend that kind of money. We can just get popcorn at the movies.

Date: Are you sure?

You: (light-headed and dreaming of a turkey sandwich)
I'm fine. Let's just go to the movies.

Example of being present (The message is: "It is good to consider me."):

Date: Would you like to go to dinner?

You: Oh, yes, I'm hungry. There is a nice, casual place next to the movies where we can get anything from a snack to a meal. So we could eat and still catch that movie.

Date: Great. I don't want to be late, but let's grab a quick bite so you won't be hungry.

Don't act as if you do not matter and then be surprised when the other person treats you as if you don't and falls for someone who does. Healthy relationships require that both people begin to let the other know who they are and what they need. Naturally, all needs could never be met by a mate, but as the relationship matures, it is important that some give-and-take on both sides occur. You may state what you want and be willing to compromise. Other times you deserve to get what you want. Someone who feels true love loves to see a partner fulfilled in this way, but also keeps a steady eye on his or her own life.

HOW TO AVOID BEING A PAIN SPONGE

◊   Fill your life with people and things you enjoyed "before" you met your mate.

◊   Develop empathy toward yourself. Do not criticize yourself more harshly than you would a friend you love. Give yourself the same encouragement and understanding you give others.

◊   Set boundaries in the area of getting involved in other people's problems too soon. Do not pay their bills, put your life on hold for them, or hold back on your own success and joy.

◊   Be supportive in a less active way—talk less and listen more. Pull back on making offers that ease daily struggles for them.

HEALTHY EMPATHY DIALOGUE

Example (Without "Doing" Anything To Help):

Date: I am so angry at my boss I could scream.

You: Oh, really? I'm sorry you're going through a rough time with him.

Date: Yeah, things are rough...(reveals details).

You: That sounds like a very difficult situation. I feel bad for you. Do you know what you are going to do next?

This example shows empathy without your having to *do* anything for your partner. It is enough to listen and to show genuine caring and concern. By leaving the results to the other person, you do not become inappropriately involved, as if the problem were really yours. As the relationship gets deeper and more committed, it is a normal part of intimacy to become more emotionally involved. But not in the beginning. Pace yourself. Go slow. If things work out, you will have all the time in the world to be tied up in knots because your partner is getting the shaft at work. For now, enjoy having only one set of problems to concern yourself with—your own.

SEX TOO SOON

Sex too soon in a relationship is a difficult mistake from which to recover. The concern today goes beyond that of the 1950s, where worries of sex "not being proper to family or church" were in the forefront. We are now well past the mid 1980s, when the age of innocence was permanently packed away. With the advent of AIDS, as well as many other sexually transmitted diseases, it has become extremely important for people to think seriously about when and with whom to share a sexual experience. There is also the emotional damage that people who have been single for years are beginning to feel.

It is time to take the phrase, "It just happened," out of our repertoire. Relationships that lead to healthy commitments and marriage are delicately balanced in the way intimacy unfolds.

Just as it is important to let a child unfold at his or her own pace, it is equally important for a relationship to unfold from a stage of innocence to maturity. The first few dates represent the Initial Phase, which can never be retrieved or recreated if it is interrupted. It is not unlike childhood, which is really your only opportunity to be innocent. It is also the only time when you may experience a taste of that all-illusive "unconditional love."

Innocence is always temporary. It is the beginning of something. Only in this Initial Phase can you have wide eyes and a completely open heart. Your lack of experience with a situation has certain advantages—not only are you more likely to be open, but you are more trusting and available for growth. Sex too soon can throw you out of this innocent stage and into experiences that can confuse and hurt you deeply.

INITIAL PHASE: 1-10 DATES

This is truly the "wonder" phase of a relationship. It is your only chance to see all good in each other and be in "unconditional like." This is what is operating when we believe we have been struck by "love at first sight." It is the initial point where you put your best foot forward and enjoy the newness, wonder, joy and awe of meeting someone whom you really like.

This phase is definitely too soon to have sex because you know very little about the other person; no matter how much it feels like you do know, you have very little knowledge of each other. Sex is revealing and personal, and if you do not have some kind of understanding about your partner, you can expect to feel some weirdness afterward. Sure it feels right at the time, but it's lust—not love—that you're feeling. And it's O.K. to feel lust within the first few dates, but if you act on it, you will be spoiling the only innocent phase that you can have with that person. Suddenly you know more about your date than is appropriate or comfortable for the amount of *time* you have known him or her. The process of intimacy did not grow slowly, but exploded into instant intimacy.

Because you cannot force intimacy before it's time, you have emotional discomfort. Imagine if children went from being 5- to 50-years old without gaining the necessary experience along the way to enable them to be successful 50-year-olds. That is what people do when they meet, go on one date and have sex.

THE AFTER-FIVE-DATES CHALLENGE

Here is the phase in which you are really becoming aware of how much you enjoy each other's company and that you might be compatible as a couple. The building blocks of a couple's ability to communicate effectively begin here. Try not to get side-tracked with sex in this stage. It is certainly easy to do because if things are going well, you have had many dates that were fun and you are beginning to talk and open up a little to each other. Allowing this phase to complete itself is in your best interest if you want a solid foundation of communication and friendship.

It is not impossible to build a good foundation after early sex, but it is extremely difficult. Sex is like a drug early on in the relationship journey. It feels great and masks problems that would begin to capture your attention if you were not intoxicated by false intimacy. Early "great sex" can distract from early danger signs that are there to help you make clear decisions about your future.

Nearly every time we have asked someone to look back to the beginning phase of what turned out to be a hideous long-term relationship and see if there were signs of the ugly demise along the way, the answer is "Yes." Indeed, there are many indications during this phase that point to future compatibility or incompatibility. You can save yourself a lot of time, trouble and heartache if you are not yet sexually involved. Your head will be clear and you will be better able to begin to see who this person is. Not only is it hard to wake up two years later in a bad relationship that consumed a great deal of your life, but it makes you less willing to be open and vulnerable again for the next relationship, which may be the right one.

MIDDLE STAGE: 11-26 DATES/THIRD MONTH

Now—and only now—are you in a good position to begin seriously discussing sexual behavior, feelings, and attitudes about sex in general. You may still want to hold off, but it's safe to begin to take that road. (For those of you who would like to wait until an engagement or marriage to have sex, this chapter is purely educational. We encourage your feelings and boundaries related to sex.)

IT IS TIME TO PROCEED TOWARD SEX WHEN:

◊   You have at least the foundation of a friendship

◊   You have some history with each other upon which to base trust

◊   You have established open and honest communication

◊   You are emotionally ready to become vulnerable

With these aspects of your relationship in place, you can communicate about sex before you have it. You can learn about each other's personality, fears, tastes and biases, which make becoming sexual less of a risk to the relationship you have created. You can talk openly about birth control, sexually transmitted diseases and what sex does and doesn't mean to you. You can also discuss your sexual preferences and boundaries with less fear.

LONGER-TERM & OTHER RELATIONSHIP STAGES: 26 DATES TO 6 MONTHS & LONGER

These stages give you the best chance for sex to become a healthy addition to your relationship, rather than a distraction. Most relationships go through a honeymoon phase in the beginning, during which everything looks rosy, and nothing the other person does annoys you. That part of the relationship is behind you and you are able to recognize and accept several traits about the other person that are irritating or unattractive. This is normal as long as your partner's negative side is not dangerous to you in any way.

Everyone has faults: Ask yourself which faults in a mate would be tolerable and which would not. It's great if your partner is in therapy and working on these things, but some issues require a lifelong journey toward emotional health, so think it over.

Since sex too early has not deluded you into thinking that Mr. Vague is Mr. Right, you can now make a clear decision about taking another step closer in the journey toward intimacy. The friendship and foundation you have achieved will get you through the difficult times—sex won't. Now, you have the opportunity to move forward or not, whatever the two of you decide together.

INCORPORATING HIM/HER INTO YOUR LIFE TOO SOON

You finally get up the courage to call that blind date and ask to meet for a cup of coffee. After three hours on the phone, during which it seems like you have everything in common, a date is made for the next night. The imagination takes over as you fantasize the ski trips you'll take together and the restaurants your new friend will surely enjoy. He or she is dreaming of how well you would get along with the family and is on the phone with them already telling them so. After the coffee date, a lunch date is made for the next day. After meeting all of his or her co-workers, lunch begins and talk of the future flows freely.

You mention to your date that you were thinking of how much she said she would love to start working out again and so you have brought her a free guest pass to your gym. You agree to meet there the next day. While working out, the two of you overhear two women discussing the bridal plans of one of them and that reminds you of the upcoming family wedding that will take place next weekend; you invite him or her to go as your date. You think to yourself, "What a good opportunity to meet my entire family along with everyone that I am remotely related to." Your newfound friend loves the idea and you make a date for the next day to go shopping for clothes.

GIVE US A BREAK!!

And we really mean a break—a break in the very unhealthy need to stay connected minute-by-minute. This is not good! If only we had a dime for every person who has said to us that as soon as they met they were inseparable, we would be very wealthy therapists. In the same way as sex too soon interrupts the natural unfolding of love, so does incorporating the new person into your life too soon. Almost always, it is a recipe for disaster.

Why do people want to rush into intimacy so quickly and become old tennis shoes to each other within a month? The answer is threefold:

1. A new relationship might feel like water in a desert.
2. If we get involved quickly, we will not see the warts.
3. We are addicted to love.

REASON #1—I'M SO THIRSTY FOR LOVE

We know that for a lot of us, searching for the right person has been a long, long road. The older we get, the more movies we see, the more singles ads we read, the more hopeless we feel. It certainly doesn't help to have so many married people commenting on what a good catch we would be and how strange it is that we haven't been caught. Naturally, we begin to worry that there is no one good left for us and that we will be alone forever.

It is not uncommon for healthy people who wish to get married some day to try to live a full life in the meantime, yet feel ever aware of an ache of loneliness. If being with someone long-term is your desire, then you long to share your life and all of its details with that one special person. When you meet someone who seems to be nice, intelligent and compatible, it is easily understandable that that you would want to glom onto that person and never let go. It feels like an oasis at last. But haven't you watched enough movies to know you're supposed to take little sips of water and not drink the whole glassful in one gulp? There is always some supporting actor there to say, "Now drink slowly—don't take in too much water too soon." We agree! No matter how quenching it seems, do not "drink in" three months of dating in three days.

THE ONE-DATE-A-WEEK RULE

There is something very important about the "one-date-a-week" process. Some might say that it is "game-playing" to regulate how often you see someone and that you should get together as often as you like. But we say that we need to be regulating most good things in our lives. Most of us try to keep a balance with food, sleep, work, play, etc. *To be healthy is to put thought into what is good for us* rather than just what feels good for the moment. You may find that events unfold in a completely different way when two lives come together slowly rather than when they are instantly locked together like suction cups. Instant love usually fades as quickly as it commences.

If the relationship is right, there will be plenty of time to meet each other's families. One cannot possibly take in the overwhelming amount of information swirling about at a family wedding without months of relating to that person beforehand.

This kind of quick incorporation amounts to relationship suicide. You are supposed to hang at their gym, see them daily, be at their workplace and know how to handle these and other daily situations—all with someone who is still a stranger! Do not underestimate the importance of the length of time spent with the person. Nothing makes up for time spent over weeks, months and years. You may be saying, "Yes, but our short time together was like a lifetime for others." Yes, it was *like* a lifetime, but it *wasn't* a lifetime—which puts you at a severe disadvantage.

Reason #2—Look Over Here & Not over There

In this scenario, whenever you meet someone, you immediately try to fit him or her into your life as soon as possible so you don't have to consider the details. What details? Details such as whether he or she is right for you, good for you, and real. Often, those with low self-esteem conduct high-speed romances to mask the negative characteristics of one or both parties. If you find yourself in intimacy races like this, you need to ask yourself why you want to miss his or her "scenery" or have him or her miss yours. Do you want to be in a relationship *so* much that you don't mind trying to fit the round peg into the square hole? No matter what he or she is really like, you may think you have seen enough in a short time to make it work. Marriage counseling is filled with questions such as: "Didn't you know this about him or her before you got married?" The answer is almost always, "Yes, but ..."

Why Do You Overlook Flaws In Your Dating Partner?

You love the high-speed chase of romance and don't want to slow down.

You don't want to see flaws and experience the disappointment of their impact.

You are uncomfortable with confrontation and prefer to pretend nothing is wrong.

You are afraid these flaws will not change and that you will have to break up.

You are sensitive and do not want to hurt your partner.

Reason #3—Might As Well Face It, You're Addicted To Love

If your pattern is that you are either very much in a relationship or you are not interested in one at all, you may be a love addict. This hot/cold pattern shows itself in extremes. If you are dating someone then you become completely involved, preoccupied and obsessed. If you are not dating someone, you tend to the rest of your life and focus on your career, hobbies or sports. But the second a relationship comes close to you, you are back into the addiction. It isn't that different from any other addiction. Love addicts focus totally on the new partnership, often hurting themselves. They may find themselves making poor decisions, which they do not usually make—unless they are "falling in love."

WHAT IS A LOVE ADDICT?

People whose involvement in romantic relationships exhibit the following patterns and behaviors are love addicts:

◊ Make decisions based on that "falling in love" feeling rather than logic and reason

◊ Fall in love easily and fall hard

◊ Drama is high and the relationships are usually complicated

◊ Focus on the "high" of the experience instead of the details of the person

◊ Look to the partner to make them feel happy and complete

◊ Abandon their own life (including family and career) so some or all of these areas suffer

◊ "Need" to be in love, instead of merely "want" to be in love

◊ Sense there is a destructive thread running through the relationship, yet continue in it

◊ Are defensive when faced with criticism of partner or the relationship

Addictions are dramatic and make us feel alive. We're attracted to someone and involved. This, of course, is not the truth. A couple like this is more "hooked" than involved. Events get complicated quickly and the need to be together and feel that "love rush" becomes all-consuming.

WHAT CAN YOU DO IF YOU RELATE TO LOVE ADDICTIONS?

1. Educate yourself through books on the subject.

2. Attend twelve-step programs specific to relationship-addiction problems (Alanon, Co-Dependents Anonymous,

Love Addicts Anonymous, etc. Local phone numbers can be found in the Yellow Pages.)

3. Consider getting psychotherapy to build self-esteem, break self-defeating patterns and understand the origin of the problem for you.

The love addict feels like half a person. In relationships, two halves do not make a "whole" but, instead, two halves make a "hole."

SUMMARY

Giving too much too soon is a tempting mistake that many of us have made or are still making. It does feel good to give to others. But when it comes to relationships, we must be willing to stay committed to finding the balance between holding back appropriately and giving appropriately. If you start out by giving too much of yourself, you run the risk of losing your self-respect and identity if the relationship does not work out. If it does work out, you run the risk of becoming depleted and resentful, as the relationship will drain you and give nothing back.

HEALTHY DATING RULE #1

Find a balance between generosity and healthy selfishness and apply the appropriate level of giving at the right time.

CHAPTER TWO

Foolish Dating Mistake # 2

YOU HOLD BACK UNTIL IT'S TOO LATE

QUIZ:

You are not giving enough information if:

1. after six dinners, your date only knows your first name.
2. you only speak when spoken to.
3. you have a "one-compliment-a-year" quota.

THE WITHHOLDER

In Chapter One we talked about giving too much in the areas of gifts, compliments, empathy, information and sex. We showed how excessiveness in any of these areas can push people away. We offered guidelines for appropriate giving during certain stages of a relationship.

Giving too much emotion can send otherwise stable, trusting people running for the hills for fear of drowning in the gushiness or the chaotic flood of your feelings, but giving too *little* emotion at each stage of a relationship creates a desperate hunger for it. The emotionally starved partner is crushed by the deprivation of emotion. What you are saying to this person is, "Don't get too close, I don't have any more to give you." The partner hungry for love and attention will leave if the deprivation is chronic. Then another perfectly acceptable partner goes down the drain because of your holding back. Most people want to give to others, but withholders are stingy because of fear of intimacy.

You tell your friends that you hold back because you are concerned about being taken advantage of, looking desperate or being rejected. You tell them that you set strong boundaries in your relationships. You are not going to "give it all away" that easily anymore. These all sound like good reasons to hold back.

THE WITHHOLDER ON A DATE

You have had three dates with the same person. You really like him or her, yet you have not uttered one compliment despite countless thoughts of attraction and admiration. You have shared no personal details about yourself. You have limited your conversation to the issue of saturated versus unsaturated fats. By the seventh date, you have shared that you have had a good time. You have revealed your profession. On the eighth date, your date confronts you about your lack of personal disclosure. You act as if you do not understand how he or she could feel that you have been distant or closed. Your date sees no point in getting together again. You feel hurt because you are interested in him or her, but you say nothing. *You held back until it was too late.*

WHAT GIVING TOO LITTLE IMPLIES

Stingy emotions can communicate to a partner that he/she is not worthy of receiving. It can reflect a "cheapskate" tendency which is a turn-off to both men and women. Being stingy damages the relationship's potential. Just as any life force needs to be nourished, watered and fed, so does a relationship between two people. The way in which this is done is to give to one another in both physical and emotional ways.

The insufficient showing of these emotional states destroys the connection. Without the sharing of emotion, there is no chance of developing a tie that will bond two people together. This is not a tie that binds or chokes or comes apart under the slightest stress but, rather, one that endures and comforts each partner.

WHAT EMOTIONAL STINGINESS SOUNDS LIKE ON A DATE

Rebecca's thoughts on the issue of holding back remind her of her experience with Barry, affectionately known by everyone as "Mr. Miser." She often wondered if the words "share" or "give" were words he even knew existed.

Here's a typical example of one of their dating encounters:

Setting: Rebecca's apartment. Barry is coming to pick her up for their seventh date. She has dressed up, wanting very much for Barry to notice. Up to this point he has given no compliments, no gifts and minimal personal information.

As she opens the door to greet him:

Barry: Hi, Rebecca. I hope you're ready. I don't want us to be late for our reservation.

Rebecca: Come in, Barry. I'll be just a minute longer. How was your day?

Barry: Thanks, but it was nothing out of the ordinary.

Rebecca: Mine was hectic, but productive. By the way, I really like the shirt you're wearing.

Barry: Thanks. Hey, we should get going. I'm hungry.

Rebecca: (dejected) Oh, O.K.

Barry was emotionally isolated and didn't even know it. Rebecca was trying to get a little personal, show a little interest in him, and give him a compliment. His responses were devoid of feeling. There just wasn't enough giving of any kind to keep Rebecca interested.

WHY DOES SOMEONE RESIST EMOTIONAL GIVING & END UP BEING STINGY?

One of the sadnesses of withholders is that they often care a lot and are very interested in their date. So why do they hold back? The most common reasons are that they

1. are afraid of rejection
2. never learned how to show their feelings
3. feel embarrassed and ashamed of their feelings
4. need to be in control
5. have a different agenda than starting a relationship
6. don't know what to do next

THE FEAR OF REJECTION—OR WHY WE HOLD BACK EXPRESSING LOVE

"Will they like and accept what I give?" "Is my giving appropriate?" "Where will this lead?" are common concerns. If someone has suffered a traumatic rejection, they can become "rejection phobic" and, as a result, avoid risks. This intense closedness can become as natural for some as being passionate can be for others. Sometimes it is fear of rejection that stops us. Our fear is that we will say, "I love you" and that our partner will fall down on the floor laughing and/or ask us to leave.

FEAR OF EMBARRASSMENT RELATED TO GIVING

If you come from a family where giving was scarce, then you never saw how it was done. If you never saw how it was done, you may feel awkward and afraid to try your hand at giving, for fear of disappointing yourself and your partner.

CONTROL ISSUES RELATED TO GIVING

If you grew up in a troubled family where things felt—and often were—chaotic, you may feel a need to keep control by burying your heart and relying strictly on your head.

HAVING AN AGENDA OTHER THAN A RELATIONSHIP

There are people who are getting into relationships left and right with no intention of finding a meaningful or lasting connection to a partner.

Anyone who has been out there in the singles jungle for more than five years can recall experiences with these types. These people make great "daters," when it comes to giving gifts or going places. But when confronted with emotional or commitment issues, poof, they're gone. It hurts to be left abruptly, just when you are wanting to get close to someone.

These dating types are not out to hurt others. They are people who may be looking to temporarily fill a void or to have a good time. Sometimes they are too young for commitment, too busy or just not interested in a committed, intimate relationship. Whatever the reason, not allowing emotional giving and sharing is hurtful, disappointing and confusing to the person who is looking for a serious relationship.

If you believe that you will be the one to change someone, you are wrong. People do not have the ability to change a withholder. These emotional "no shows" must see the problem in themselves, recognize the destructiveness of such behavior in a relationship and begin to change toward being more giving.

A more constructive response to withholding partners is to leave them and find someone who is available. Whether you are dating a withholder or *you* are the withholder, recognizing the fatality of such behavior is crucial to a successful relationship.

TYPES OF EMOTIONAL GIVING IN RELATIONSHIPS

The varied ways one can give emotionally to a partner are:

1. showing empathy
2. showing interest in him or her
3. showing love, and
4. showing anger, sadness and fear.

These are emotional areas of a relationship that, if expressed, deepen the friendship, encourage romance and create intimacy.

THE IMPORTANCE OF SHOWING EMPATHY IN YOUR RELATIONSHIPS

Webster's dictionary defines empathy as:

the identification with or vicarious experience of the feelings, thoughts of another.

This means when your date tells you that his or her mother is ill, you genuinely care and are able to show it. You *do not* say, "Gee, I'm in the mood for a good comedy and a giant pizza." Rather, you say, "I am so sorry to hear that. I know how I felt when my Dad was sick. It was very hard on me. I feel for what you are going through." When all else fails, use the following tried-and-true empathic dialogue; *"Oh, I am sorry. Is there anything I can do?"* Don't say it if you don't mean it, but many times we feel it and just do not know how to put it into a simple offering of help.

WITHHOLDING OF EMPATHY IN RELATIONSHIPS

For many people, the above words of support seem too emotional, too intimate. Not saying anything or changing the subject is more comfortable. People hold back empathy mainly because they are:

1. scared
2. cut off from their own emotions
3. controlling

Scared people are afraid of looking weak or being taken advantage of. They fear that if they start connecting emotionally with their partner, the relationship will turn too serious. They would rather keep exchanges light and fun and avoid intimacy.

Emotionally stunted people don't feel very much at all. They have defense mechanisms that separate them from feeling their life. They might tell you that they won the lottery with as much emotion as if they were telling you that they just bought a "TV Guide" at the drug store. Keeping their feelings under control makes them feel safe. It is almost impossible to fight with them, feel passion with them or get to know them.

Controlling people are concerned with many feelings. They are usually very sensitive people. They will let you express your feelings but they won't react. Their goal, which usually is unconscious, is to feel removed, unaffected by your emotion. This is how they stay in control. They leave their dates hurt and confused, which is the reason most of these people receive poison pen letters from former lovers on Valentine's Day.

If you are dating a person who cannot give you empathy, *run, don't walk* away as fast as you can, or you will get hurt. If this section reads like your autobiography, you must perfect the following guidelines:

PERSONAL SKILLS OF INTIMACY

1. Start listening for the "feeling content" when people talk to you. Listen more and talk less.

2. Ask questions that encourage people to share more of the emotional details of their situations. Try to relate to them.

3. Remember a time in your childhood when you were scared or sad. Sit down and write a paragraph about what happened to you.

4. Force yourself to use "feeling" words when you speak, such as these: angry, hurt, sad, happy, confused, irritated, bored, interested, worried, secure, serene, anxious, excited, etc.

HOW TO DEAL WITH A PARTNER WHO WITHHOLDS EMPATHY

INSUFFICIENT EMPATHY DIALOGUES

George and Ellen have been dating for one year. George took a new, high-stress job seven months ago and has been talking about the stress of the new position ever since.

George: Ellen, I am still so stressed.

Ellen: I know you are, George. I feel bad seeing you like this. We have talked about your alternatives, and a lot about how bad this is for you. Is there anything I can do to help you at this point?

George: That is what I really like about you, Ellen. You are so nice and understanding. You never make me feel pressured.

Ellen: I am glad to be here for you and talk about this job situation of yours anytime. But I also need to know if we can make some time for talk about us. I never feel like it is a good time.

George: Ellen, I am very stressed and confused about things. I have a lot on my mind.

George doesn't seem to care at all about Ellen's feelings. Ellen shows a healthy amount of empathy toward George and his situation, but he is too wrapped up in himself to tend to her feelings. He is selfish and unable to show empathy.

People with adequate self-esteem would be angry at someone like George. They would feel the inequality and insensitivity in the communication. They would probably leave the relationship or withdraw from being empathic and generous with their support.

Appropriate Empathy Dialogues

Learning how to strike a balance between showing empathy and taking care of your own feelings is an important relationship survival tool. Here is a healthy version of George's response to Ellen:

George: I am stressed and confused about my life. I am not sure what I want or can do about it.

Ellen: George, I can see you are upset. However, I am going through a hard time myself. We have been dating for a year and I often feel as if it is never a good time to bring up some of the stuff that I need to talk to you about.

George: I apologize, Ellen. I have been so focused on myself, I have been leaning on you and the relationship. What is up with you? Let's go to dinner and I will listen.

Ellen: That's great George. I feel better.

George shows empathy to Ellen. In doing so, he is able to be honest about his poor behavior, to understand how Ellen must feel and to commit to trying to change. He shows that he cares about her by making her feelings important. When you are a sufficient empathizer, you communicate, "I am a caring person and I can be there for you when you need me." Believe it or not, most people are more attracted to Mr. and Ms. Warmth than they are to Mr. or Ms. Abdominal Ripple. If you have Dating Mistake #2 as a problem, trade in your morning at the gym for a moment to *feel* your life and the lives of those around you.

HOLDING BACK INTEREST IN YOUR PARTNER

People feel complimented and happy when you tell them you're interested in them. It is a validating experience. With this in mind, it doesn't make sense to keep this positive information from our dating partners. If you like someone, tell them; if they like you as well, the relationship is off to a positive start. On the other hand, if you express interest and it is not returned, you won't melt or disappear. You will feel disappointed, but you'll survive.

WHY PEOPLE WITHHOLD SHARING OF INTEREST IN ANOTHER PERSON

Remember those high school days when letting someone know you were interested in them was too terrifying for words? You used to beg your friends not to tell anyone that you liked someone. You did this because you just "knew" that person could never be interested in you. You felt sure you would be humiliated.

But why would anyone, man or woman, be insulted if someone shows an interest? If they, too, felt interested, some of the pressure of getting together would be lessened. If they were not interested in that person, they could be polite and explain that they aren't pursuing more interaction. Healthy people can appreciate the compliment in having someone interested in them.

REVEALING DIALOGUE

An appropriate expression of interest is:

Linda: I really enjoyed tonight. I hope we can do it again soon.

A "holding back" expression of interest is:

Linda: The movie was good. Thanks for taking me.

Both responses are "nice" and "appropriate" but the first example shows more feeling and enthusiasm and alludes to the future. The second expression is factual and polite, but leaves room for confusion and negative interpretation.

EARLY STAGES OF A RELATIONSHIP & SHOWING INTEREST

It is possible in the early stages of a relationship to show a person you are interested in him or her without sounding as if you are making a life-long commitment. There is quite a difference between:

"I think you're great" and
"Will you spend eternity with me? Please never leave my side."

The expression of positive feelings toward your partner is an encouraging gesture. The showing of excessive interest too soon can be suspicious and off-putting. "Never leave my side" is dramatic and spooky; it smacks of a scene from the movie, "Fatal Attraction." But a light and positive comment makes us and our dates feel good inside and encourages a move closer together.

MIDDLE STAGE OF A RELATIONSHIP & SHOWING INTEREST

This is the make-it or break-it stage, the time to start getting more specific about what interests you in your dating partner. This is when people start seriously thinking about how well they get along, and how compatible they are. The expression of interest during this stage evolves from a superficial to a deeper level. These deeper expressions of what interests you about your partner open the door for your partner to explore his or her level of interest in you. If interest at this stage is based on your bulging wallet, I.Q. scores, or supermodel statistics, the relationship is fragile. If someone is continuing to date you steadily through the middle stages of a relationship just because of some external "dating asset," interest will wane when they get to know "you the person" rather than "you the object."

If you are dating with only a superficial level of interest in someone by the middle stages of a relationship, consider ending it. Real intimacy (not just casual dating) requires mutual expressions of interest in the deeper aspects of each other. Don't get us wrong— money is great, good looks are fun and a strong mind all enhance a relationship. These traits *are* of interest to most of us. However, without a deeper, more mature level of interest in a person's feelings, wants, needs and sensibilities, a relationship has little chance of making it through the middle stage.

Later Stages of a Relationship and Showing Interest

Showing an interest in a person keeps the chemistry going. It also strengthens your bond and can take it to new heights, even beyond the crests of the earlier "honeymoon" stage.

Relationships can get stale, even after six months. When people begin to feel invisible or taken-for-granted, they are tempted to take drastic measures to get attention. How would you like it if your partner of six months dyed his or her hair green and started stripping in public to get your attention? People can get so hungry for attention that they prefer negative attention over no attention at all. You can avoid this kind of desperate act by not withholding expressions of interest in your partner.

HEALTHY GUIDELINES FOR SHOWING INTEREST

BEGINNING STAGE

Dates 1-10   Healthy message to partner sounds like: "I'm having a great time. Let's get together more often."

MIDDLE STAGE

Dates 11-15   Healthy message to partner sounds like: "I want to learn more about you."

EARLY COMMITMENT STAGE

Dates 16-25   Healthy message to partner sounds like: "I care about you a lot and want to see only you."

LONGER-TERM STAGE

Dates 26 on   Healthy message to partner sounds like: "I am interested in moving forward and making more of a commitment."

HOLDING BACK LOVE VS. EXPRESSING LOVE TOO SOON

At the end of John's third date with Lynn, he pauses and looks deeply into her eyes and says, "I love you." For that particular move, John receives the "Foolish Dating Mistake" Booby Prize. No! No! No! love stuff yet! (See Chapter One.) John doesn't love Linda yet. He doesn't really know her. Who is she to him at this point? Probably nothing more than someone whom he thinks he must have to be happy but, in reality, she may be the worst possible match for him.

Lucky for John, Linda was healthier than he was. Her reply was:

John, I barely know you. Being in love with you at this point isn't possible for me. Please slow down. (This is the nice version.)

Note that Lynn isn't holding back love. She is being mature and realistic. (You are holding back love when, after significant time and experience has been shared, you "feel" love and you consciously withhold it from your partner.)

Love Defined

The Webster's Dictionary definition of love is:

a feeling of warm personal attachment or deep affection

With this definition in mind, it should be clear that *you are not in love in the early stages of a relationship!* Don't you feel relieved? No matter how strongly you may feel about someone, if you have just met him or her, don't even dream about saying you're in love. Healthy people will instantly disappear from your life. Instead of thinking about love, think more about what you want to wear on the next date or where you are going to eat.

What Is Love, Anyway? How Do You Know When You Are In Love?

These are the questions that haunt all of us who are in search of lasting love. Knowing when "like" turns into "love" isn't an easy process. Knowing when and if love is enough in order to consider making a lasting commitment is another part of the relationship dilemma. Love involves respect and deep caring. It involves a genuine desire to give to another person, to outwardly verbalize love and act in loving ways. Love involves commitment, the sticking by someone during difficult times, with a full effort to make things work. Love involves friendship and elements of romantic and physical attraction.

The words "attachment" and "deep" used in Webster's definition indicate a significant experience that has endured over a period of time. In the beginning of a relationship a strong liking or interest in someone is all you need. In the later stages of a relationship, mature love can develop.

Confusing Expectations About Love

Associated with expressing love is the concern about expectations. What are we supposed to do now? Do we move in together, get engaged, elope, tell the world, buy each other expensive gifts? Relax. *Love is just a feeling to be expressed.* Yes, it can lead to any or all of the above. However, in the beginning, just enjoy it, don't be afraid of it. Take the pressure off yourself. See the admission of loving someone as the beginning of a new, deeper stage of the relationship instead of seeing it as a marriage proposal. You are not signing a contract by admitting love, but *not* admitting it can kill any chances of its working out. In the 1997 movie, "My Best Friend's Wedding," the lead female character resists fully acknowledging to herself and her best friend—a man— that she has loved him for nine years. When she finds out he is getting married, she admits her feelings to herself and to him, but it is too late. He has strong friendship feelings for her, but has fallen in love with someone else. He waited and pined for years, and then moved on. Lucky for him, unlucky for our female "withholder of love." At the movie, we cried for her because she lost something wonderful—because of her fears and her need to stay invulnerable.

EXPRESSING LOVE DIALOGUES

Linda: I'm so happy that we met and started dating. I want you in my life for a very long time. I love you very much.

This communication includes compliments, feelings, thoughts about the future and the expression of love. Would you feel safe opening up to a partner who expressed their feelings in this way?

Example of exchange in which holding back the expression of love negatively skews the possibilities:

Linda: I realize how safe and happy I feel with you. I have been having a wonderful time in this relationship and want you in my life for a long time. I love you very much.

Bob (the Withholder):
I have been having fun too, Linda, and I have special feelings for you.

Linda: (thinking to herself, "Special feelings? What does that mean? Sister, friend, future wife?")

This vignette indicates that Linda loves Bob. We are assuming that Bob also loves Linda. He is being polite and positive. By not saying, "I love you," however, Bob confuses and discourages her.

When you hold back expressing love and saying, "I love you," until it's too late, you may wind up losing the love of your life and live to regret it. Don't be afraid of love. The pain of losing a desirable partner may be worse and longer-lasting than taking a chance by saying those three words to the person you love.

HOLDING BACK ANGER

Holding powerful negative feelings inside can cause depression, headaches and hair loss (we bet that got your attention).

Remember the last time you told yourself, "Don't tell him/her you're mad. It will mess up the evening. Forget it." (At which point your temples felt as if they were exploding and every little thing he/she did—from walking to breathing—irritated you.)

Holding these feelings inside creates a wall between you and your partner. Your first thought regarding the issue of showing anger might be that it is smart *not* to show it. It is a precarious situation to express anger at someone you are dating, someone in whom you are interested and whose interest you would like returned. But don't get frustrated. Here are some tips.

DESTRUCTIVE EXPRESSION OF ANGER

Here is an example of "blasting" your partner with anger to the degree that he or she may wonder about your mental stability:

I am furious—enraged—at you for being late! You are an inconsiderate louse!

If you are angry at your date's tardiness, you should let him or her know. Why? Because if you don't, he or she will not have learned that being late is a major negative button for you. He/she may even do it again. When we let someone know that we are angry at them for something, we create the opportunity for them to stop doing it. It is crucial to intimacy to know how your behavior affects your partner.

Constructive Expression of Anger

Anger has gotten a lousy rap. People consider it negative. Anger is negative when it is expressed abusively or inappropriately. It is constructive when the goal is to let someone know us more intimately, even if it is about what makes us angry.

You can say something like:

Our reservations are for 7 p.m. I know sometimes you run late and it is not a huge deal, but I would love it if you would try to be on time. It means a lot to me.

The confrontation doesn't have to be long and should *not* be an attack on the person, but instead a statement about the behavior and how you feel about it.

Common Reasons to Feel Anger in a Relationship are:

1. inconsiderate behavior by your partner
2. stinginess
3. possessiveness
4. competitiveness
5. betrayal (sexual or otherwise)
6. abuse

In any of these situations, anger would be a normal reaction. If your partner takes the last eclair from the tray without asking you if you want it, you may feel irritated. You could overlook this because it's insignificant unless you harbor resentment, hoping that the eclair is stale. If thoughts like this occur, you should express your feelings before they turn into hostility.

If you were to express the anger immediately, you might avoid such an uncharacteristic thought and, instead, say, "I would have liked to have had the eclair before you snatched it up. Maybe you could offer some of it to me next time."

This response lets your date know how you feel and gives him or her a chance to change behavior or apologize. This is much better for the relationship than having cruel revenge fantasies.

Expressing Anger Over Important Issues

When the issues get bigger than eclairs, it can get scarier to express the anger. It can be very uncomfortable to confront people about something you want that they are not giving you (emotionally or physically). It can be unsettling to have to state how mad you are at them. Part of the difficulty may be the fear of retaliation. Or that they will think you are petty. Another concern might be hurting their feelings. And then there is always the thought that maybe we have no real right to be angry.

We have been told by clients that they are afraid of their anger, afraid of losing control. Others say they fear their anger will be judged or dismissed.

These obstacles to expressing anger at your partner can be worked through in some of the following ways:

1. Learn about why it is so hard for you to express anger.

2. Try to identify the hurt that is underneath the anger exactly when you are feeling it. Think before you talk.

3. Make your self-respect more important than any person or any relationship. Build your self-esteem by developing standards and rules of behavior and assertively presenting them to your partner.

4. Remind yourself that anger is only a feeling. Catastrophic results usually don't happen just because you get mad. Practice expressing anger with someone who cares about you, someone you trust.

Anger Can Heal Your Relationship

There is no chance for the healing and forgiveness to begin without going through the anger process. When you say to your partner, "You have lied and cheated and I am so mad at you I could scream. I don't know what I'm going to do. I am blind with anger," the relationship can progress from there in an honest way. If you suppress the anger, your partner may never know how you feel. This removes the possibility for amends to occur and trust to begin to rebuild. Withholding anger is a "Foolish Dating Mistake" because it creates dishonesty and distance.

No matter at what stage the relationship is, expressing your anger is appropriate.

GUIDELINES FOR EXPRESSING ANGER

If something happens on the first date, simply say, "I feel angry," or "That made me mad." If you hold back at the first stage, you run the risk of being treated like a doormat. You also miss the opportunity to show your date how to communicate with you.

If you hold back in the *middle stages*, you are in the midst of playing a manipulation game. The game goes like this: "My lack of temper and expectations will endear me forever to this person. Then when I snag him/her, I can let him/her know what bugs me." This is a great reason for someone to dump you down the road. If he or she thought you were a gentle breeze of a person, how shocked they will be to find out you can be a hurricane.

If you are left because you expressed your anger consistently and appropriately, be thankful that you are out of that relationship. Holding in your anger to avoid conflict with an unreasonable partner will hurt you emotionally. Are they really worth it? We hope you say "No" at this point, and begin to embrace the positive aspects of expressing anger and all other feelings in your relationships.

SUMMARY

Holding back until it is too late is a "Foolish Dating Mistake" that gnaws at people for years. "If I had only said I loved him/her or, if only I had let my anger out before it turned hostile, we could still be together." These are common regrets. If you can learn to give and share your emotional self, someone has a real opportunity to know, love and commit to you.

HEALTHY DATING RULE #2

Express your feelings and thoughts openly with your partner as soon as it is appropriate.

CHAPTER THREE

Foolish Dating Mistake # 3

⸱⸺☙

YOU FOCUS TOO MUCH ON PHYSICAL CHEMISTRY

QUIZ:

Do you:

1. get more excited watching your date's backside than when he/she is walking toward you?
2. know that if your date doesn't look like a model for bikinis or Speedos, you're out of the pool?
3. think age destroys a person's looks?

Part of this foolish mistake is the belief in certain romantic myths about love ....

MYTH #1—IF YOU DO NOT FEEL LOVE AT FIRST SIGHT, YOU WILL NEVER LOVE THAT PERSON ENOUGH TO BE REALLY HAPPY WITH THEM.

> He never loved but loved at first sight.
>
> —from "As You Like It" by William Shakespeare

This makes no sense at all. We have often wanted to confront Shakespeare for originating this myth, which continues down through the ages in the face of much evidence to the contrary each day in therapists' offices throughout the country.

What if the moment you meet your future love you have a stomachache? That could be a little distracting. Or maybe they remind you of someone who once hurt you? But in time, you are able to see them for who they really are. Love-at-first-sight was concocted as an appealing idea on many levels. It sounds so easy and it's fast, exciting and romantic. Most of the time, however, love-at-first-sight turns out to be nothing more than a strong physical attraction to someone—an attraction that will fade in time into a more realistic form of relating (or not).

MYTH #2—IT IS IMPORTANT TO LOOK YOUR BEST AT ALL TIMES FOR YOUR PARTNER OR HE/SHE WILL LEAVE

This one gives us a headache every time we hear it. Who looks good all the time? There are many situations, such as moving day, when it should be illegal to look great. Just because someone does not happen to look great all the time, it should not send his or her partner prowling the streets for a new mate.

MYTH #3—GOOD LOOKS ARE ALL THAT MAKE A RELATIONSHIP EXCITING.

People who believe this are superficial, uncreative, boring and probably below average in the sensuality department. This is a very naive, immature conception of attraction between individuals. So many things can make a relationship really special, including humor, loyalty, spontaneity and attitude.

MYTH #4—IF YOU ARE NOT INTENSELY PHYSICALLY ATTRACTED TO A PERSON INITIALLY, YOU WILL NEVER BE.

This is like the love-at-first-sight myth, except it addresses physical chemistry instead of the feeling of love. This is also an immature concept. Attraction is a process and many things can develop over time to affect what draws us to a person. We change and they change and so attraction can change.

MATURE LOVE

Mature love creates excitement, but not the kind that depletes us. Mature love presents adventure and challenge to its partners. People involved in mature love relationships are realistic and are as interested in peacefulness and comfort as they are in excitement. This kind of love allows people to enjoy each other. Mature relationships have conflict, but each partner is invested in resolution so they can resume enjoying the relationship. The more acquainted the partners become with each other, the more they like each other.

IMMATURE LOVE

Immature love is fragile. It is based on fantasy, superficiality and competitiveness. People involved in such relationships are usually insecure and selfish. The main motivation for being in the relationship is for the drama. These relationships fluctuate between intensely romantic and satisfying to argumentative and stressful. People cannot seem to live with or without each other. The more acquainted they become, the more the conflict escalates.

Focusing too much on looks and not enough on the whole person is a mistake that you must stop making. This mistake is causing you to miss out on many opportunities for fulfilling, intimate relationships. It brings to mind a conversation that author/therapist Lila Gruzen once had with "Mark" in her office about his romantic life. He had recently had a first date with a woman that he was excited about. As he put it, "There was a tremendous attraction" (a requirement for Mark before he would even consider asking a woman for a date). The in-session conversation went as follows:

Lila: Hi Mark. How are you tonight and what would you like to share with me about your week?

Mark: (looking depressed) I had a second date with Allison. (pause)

Lila: Well, how'd it go? I know you were looking forward to it.

Mark: I was not attracted to her. I realized this minutes into the date.

Lila: Do you have any idea why the attraction disappeared?

Mark: Yeah. The night I met her she had this tight little black dress
            on and she looked really hot and thin. This week we went
            out for a daytime date and she wore shorts and a hat. Her
            thighs looked bigger and I really hate hats.

Lila: (thinking to herself) Based on this response, Mark and I
            should pre-schedule weekly appointments to meet until at
            least the year 2020.

Mark is over-focused on appearance. In fact, the main source of
chemistry for Mark is limited to how someone looks. We wonder
how many of you out there are reading this and saying to yourself,
"So what's wrong with that? It's the same for me." Well, welcome
to the perfect Foolish Dating Mistakes chapter for you!

CHEMISTRY COUNTS, BUT IT'S NOT EVERYTHING

Don't get us wrong, chemistry is an important component of an
intimate relationship. In fact, one of the benefits of being in a
relationship is enjoying the excitement and romance of an attraction.
But not all attractions are "intense" nor do they need to be. Some
start out minimally and have the potential to grow in intensity. The
person who is obsessed with physical appearance *has* to have the
intensity and has to have it right away in order to be open to
pursuing a relationship.

People who hold these beliefs are "love addicts" or "fantasy
addicts." For people like this, a relationship becomes nothing more
than the pursuit of a "high." It also becomes a way for them to try to
raise their self-esteem. Through the pursuit of someone they
perceive as close to perfect, they feel more valuable themselves. It is
similar to the use of alcohol. Some people drink occasionally to
relax or be social, while others drink to get drunk so they can feel
more confident with themselves. Some people look to relationships
for intimacy and stability, while others look for drama.

THE GREEKS ON LOVE

The Greeks talked about the existence of many different kinds of
love. Eros and Mania are two kinds of love that people who are

obsessed with appearance seek to create. Eros is the romantic, sexual, sensual type of love, characterized by a love-at-first-sight feeling accompanied by definite physiological reactions. Manic love is characterized by possessiveness, jealousy, and stressful love that alternates between irrational joy and anxiety to depression and pain.

Although aspects of Eros and Mania are exciting and an attractive part of a new relationship, they can be destructive when taken too far. This type of chemistry does not lead to intimacy, but to drama and chaos. In mature relationships, the obsessive kind of attraction begins to settle down. So things evolve from:

"I couldn't take my eyes off his coal black eyes" to
"He is cute, but more important, he's bright and caring."

In immature love, the beginning stage sounds like:

"I can't think, sleep or eat. All I do is keep picturing her gorgeous body in my mind."

In immature love, the later stages sound like:

"I can't think about anything except her gorgeous body."

There is no growth beyond the superficial level with immature love.

THE PURSUIT OF HEALTHY CHEMISTRY

A stark difference exists between the average person seeking physical chemistry in their relationship and the person obsessed with physical chemistry. The average person does not need physical perfection or the fulfillment of an immature fantasy to be content. You will not hear the average person say, "He was so handsome, but his hair was receding and I don't want to be stuck with a bald guy some day." But such a declaration is common for the chemistry-obsessed person. They truly believe that the only way they will be able to sustain chemistry is for their partner to remain "perfect." On one level they're right, because the person obsessed with looks has no clue as to how to develop intense attraction based on other traits. For them, chemistry equals looks.

The average person who seeks a chemical attraction with a partner is also seeking companionship and intimacy. They are aware that looks change, and that in the long run other attributes make or break a relationship. This is a mature way to look at love and relationships.

Mature people also know something that is very important:

Most of us do not have glamour magazines pursuing our faces for their covers and offering us big bucks for such a spread. The reason for this is that most of us are not physically gorgeous. Most of us are average. We each establish our own appeal through the use of style, confidence and working with whatever God has given us.

Interestingly, most people who are obsessed with the looks of their partner are only average looking themselves. Remember Mark? He was an average looking guy with an average personality, yet he obsessively required that the women he dated look beautiful at all times. Mark is an insecure man. Lila's session with Mark continued to focus on his date with Allison; he remained focused on the issue of her appearance, despite Lila's attempts to broaden his perspective on her:

Lila: What else attracted you to Allison at your initial meeting?

Mark: I guess I liked the fact that she looked better than any of the girls my friends were with. I felt proud. I assumed she always looked hot.

Lila: I recall your telling me that first night that you found her funny and bright.

Mark: I did? Are you sure?

At this point in the conversation, Lila was tempted to take one of three actions:

1. Get out of the chair and whack Mark on the side of his head.
2. Charge him triple the fee for the headache he's causing her.
3. Feel a deep empathy for him and his intimacy problems.

The latter reaction definitely won out. We struggle to help the "Marks" of the world connect with the whole person instead of only her "body." He had been complaining for more than a year that he longed for an intimate relationship, yet every time he met someone he found a reason to reject her (usually because of something related to lack of sustained chemistry). Mark suffers from the inability to relate to love relationships in a mature way. He is the type of man who is stuck in adolescence, thinking of a partner as a sex object or social ornament instead of a friend and companion as well. Mark is the type of man who might choose to create a sexual encounter with his partner as a way of avoiding a problem or a conflict.

REASONS WHY OVER-FOCUSING ON APPEARANCE WRECKS A RELATIONSHIP

1. It can intoxicate you and blind you to potential problems.
2. When fluctuations in appearance occur, it can create major conflict.
3. It can create too much focus and pressure on sexual intimacy.
4. It limits the range of your sensuality.

OVEREMPHASIS ON PHYSICAL CHEMISTRY CAN BLIND YOU TO PROBLEMS

Phil could not stop thinking about how beautiful Kathy was. Although they had had only two dates, he felt like he was "in love." Some of Phil's friends knew Kathy through mutual friends and they didn't like her very much. She had proved to be a gossip and was mean-spirited at times. When they shared their feelings with Phil, he got mad at them.

Phil: You guys are jealous of her. She's prettier than any of your girlfriends. You wish you could have her.

John: Are looks all you think about? She talks behind everyone's back, even yours, I hear.

Phil: She is probably just trying to be friendly. She is shy.

Phil's friends do not know whether to laugh or to cry at this comment. What is wrong with their friend? Kathy is known as the "Wicked Witch Of The East" in their social circle. Why doesn't Phil trust them? Why is he so blinded by her?

Several weeks later, Phil is confronted by a long-time friend.

Mike: Phil, Kathy is telling everybody that you're cheap. She says she has to hint and beg to get you to take her out for dinner. The latest joke about this is that you have more discount coupons than dollars in your wallet.

Phil: What? Are you kidding. I thought I was treating her well. I have been feeling so lucky to be with her...How could I have been so wrong about her?

Phil had forgotten to spend time getting to know Kathy as a person. He became obsessed with how great-looking she was and fantasized that everything else about her was great, too. It was devastating to find out that she was not very nice.

Phil has low self-esteem. He feels unattractive and insecure. Being with an attractive woman is one of the ways that he has tried to improve his self-image. When we feel unattractive, our motivation to pursue a particular partner may be based on the positive attention we receive because of that partner's looks. This is the wrong reason to date someone.

APPEARANCES FLUCTUATE & IMMATURE RELATIONSHIPS OFTEN CRUMBLE

Rita was looking great these days. She had been working out a lot and had recently bought a lot of nice clothes. She met Craig at a singles mixer and he was really taken by her. Craig told one of his friends, "I met the girl of my dreams." He asked Rita out and they both anticipated their first date with excitement.

Scene: Rita's apartment. She is looking in the mirror with horror at her new hairdo. She wanted to look wild and exciting for Craig, so she had her hair cut and permed. As she glares at herself in the mirror, she is reminded of a troll doll with it's hand in a live lamp socket. She hoped her hot, tight black dress would compensate for the hair horror...

Rita: (the bell rings, she opens the door,)
       Hi! Craig. It's great to see you!

Craig: (At seeing her, he is also thinking of troll dolls and excuses to run out and buy her a large hat.)
       Hi, Rita...

Rita: Come on in. Have you decided where we're going tonight?

Craig: How about if we stay in and order take-out?

Craig is on automatic "Get me out of this relationship" mode. He is an expert at immature love. He has lost interest in Rita because of the change in her appearance. He doesn't want to get to know her because at this moment he isn't attracted to her. He is the type of guy who would really struggle with the attraction issue when his wife got pregnant, or when his girlfriend developed acne during a stressful period at work.

Women are just as prone to this kind of immature response to change in a man's appearance. Like the woman who thought her date was actually taller than he turned out to be and she subsequently told her friends, "He was really cute, but he must have been wearing shoes with heels the night we met because he was so much shorter than I remembered. I was looking right into his eyes when we were dancing. I can't have that, I have to look up to the man I dance with to feel attracted to him." Wow, please push the delete button on this type of thinking.

Appearances change. Bad perms, outbursts of acne, weight changes, and bad clothes can change Cinderella into "the girl next door," but why not check her out, anyway? After all, since she is right next door, what's wrong with a little convenience instead of the pursuit of an illusive fantasy? And who needs Prince Charming if the boy next door is waiting to sweep you off of your feet?

Chemistry addicts become addicted to an image and that image is rigidly fixed on beauty and fantasy. Any alteration in this fantasy can cause a drastic change in feelings for your former "love prize." So when you meet a guy and he's wearing a tuxedo, and the next time he takes you out he is wearing plaid baggies and a T-shirt, you might feel "repulsed" by him. You might also feel anger. How dare he ruin the fantasy that you set in your mind after that first meeting.

As exaggerated as this scenario may sound, it is not. Year after year we see people who are unable to transcend fluctuations in the appearance of their partners. They are unable to maintain attraction without the constancy of the physical and romantic fantasy.

TOO MUCH FOCUS ON SEX

What goes along with an over-focus on looks is an over-focus on sex. This over-focus leads to having sex way too soon in the relationship. In Chapters One and Two we discussed how having sex too soon can ruin the chances for healthy intimacy. It is difficult to have a relationship with the whole person when you are obsessing about their "body parts"—and this is what the person obsessed with sex does. In conversations it sounds something like this:

Tom: Tell me about your date with Mary?

Bob: She has the most beautiful legs.

Tom: Well, that's great. What did you guys do?

Bob: I stared at her long legs and she seemed to have fun too.

Tom: What does she do for a living?

Bob: I didn't ask. I bet she was busy checking me out, too. I think 'it' might happen on the next date.

Bob sounds immature. Bob sounds obsessive. Bob sounds boring. He is stuck on one note. This thinking process creates the kind of sexual tension that causes people to act out sexually before the appropriate time. Bob is the kind of date whose right hand may be making its way up your thigh at record speed while you're attempting to tell him about your day.

The female version of Bob might sound like:

Rhonda: How was your date with Chet?

Laura: Great. He has the most muscular arms I have ever seen.

Rhonda: What did you guys do on your date?

Laura: He wanted to go out to dinner, but I suggested we just walk along the beach because I wanted any excuse just to touch his muscles.

Rhonda: Do you think he's a nice guy?

Laura: I'll bet he's a great lover.

Men and women who become intoxicated by their dates' looks, are not fully available for the whole experience. Talking, making decisions together, playing, relaxing are all activities in which looks make no difference. These are the activities that make up a date that allows people to start the process of getting to know each other as people, not just as sexual ornaments.

For those of you who are tired and worried over why you're still single, the importance of resisting overindulgence in the physical aspects of a person in the beginning of a relationship in order to improve the odds of it working out cannot be stressed enough—like it or not.

The Evolution of a Physical Appearance Addict

The main causes for this type of behavior and attitude in a relationship are:

1. low self-esteem
2. insecurities
3. perfectionism
4. fear of intimacy

Low Self-esteem

People with low self-esteem are not emotionally free to make choices for themselves based on how those choices feel to them. Instead, they base them on how they look and sound to other people. They do this because they desperately want approval and are very careful to choose what they believe would bring positive attention to themselves. It would be too risky for someone with very low self-esteem to go out with someone whom they see as flawed for fear that they would be ridiculed by others. Acceptance by others becomes more important than their own happiness. In fact, approval and acceptance are so important that many people with low self-esteem do not know themselves well enough to make an accurate choice in any major area of their life.

Improvement of self-esteem was discussed in Chapter One. The guidelines for building self-esteem are worth memorizing and practicing in order to become maturely tolerant in the areas of appearance and chemistry in your relationships.

PERFECTIONISM

Many people suffer from perfectionism. It is not a happy way to live. Perfectionists have difficulty accepting any deviation from a standard they have deemed necessary for things to function as they feel they should. By keeping things perfect, perfectionists can fool themselves into thinking that everything is going to work out just fine. This is their way of trying to control their world and manage their anxiety.

The perfectionist looks at a hair out of place and starts having distorted thoughts like, "Boy, that woman is ugly" or "I'll bet she's a slob" or "He must not care about me or himself if he can look like that." The perfectionist may *believe* that he/she is looking for a mate, but his/her *behavior* indicates that the person has not been born yet who will be able to measure up.

FEAR OF GETTING CLOSE

Getting close and being rejected is a common and frightening prospect for many people. Past hurts, low self-esteem and other sources of insecurity keep us from being relaxed and flexible in our approach to finding a partner. Yet, if we keep focusing on the body, we are bound to find a reason to withdraw our attention and affection. Our bodies change and do things that are not always within our control. Yet some people literally cannot recover their attraction to someone after they have heard that person pass gas!

"They just didn't seem romantic after that. Too much reality— who needs that? I will just start over with someone new," are typical reactions. *Believe us, this really happens.*

Overcoming the fear of intimacy can help the physical-appearance junkie develop and maintain attraction to real people with imperfect bodies. If you can feel better about yourself and stop playing the unconscious game of "I'll dump you before you dump me," maybe you still have a chance to attain intimacy in a relationship. *If you stop being so picky, your partner may follow your lead and relax his or her rigid standards as well; then you can let your stomach pooch a little without being stressed about it!*

CREATING CHEMISTRY

The real key to changing this pattern of appearance-focused relationships comes in learning new skills for building chemistry. We need to take the "magicalness" out of chemistry between partners and understand that we have an active part in its existence and its growth.

GUIDELINES FOR CREATING CHEMISTRY	
Focus On The Positive	Make a list of the person's positive traits. Write down positive goals for your relationship.
Create Interesting & Exciting Encounters	Meet at a romantic restaurant. Go to a place that is new to both of you. Express and participate in each other's fantasies.
Visualize The Type Of Life You Want & Try To Fit The Person You Are Dating Into That Picture	Imagine traveling to many new places. See your partner by your side—helping you, enjoying adventures and having fun.
Avoid Being Overly Analytical About The Person You Are With	Feel more; think less.
Focus On One Physical Aspect Of The Person That Is Attractive	If she has pretty hair, look at it, touch it. If he has attractive eyes, look into them directly. Enjoy these qualities. Do not compare him/her with others.
Become More Sensual—Utilize Your Five Senses	Chemistry based on sight alone is fragile and limited. Focus on perfume, cologne, sound of voice, feel of skin, as well as looks.
Focus On What Honestly Makes You Feel Happy	Take an inventory on what has made you happy in the past. Be aware of your emotional needs and focus on how your partner fulfills those needs.

SUMMARY

A person's appearance is a small part of his/her identity. People embody so many facets that are attractive and seductive. Learning to explore the different aspects of people is important in the development of chemistry in relationships. Even more important than learning about your potential partner, however, is the ability to explore creatively your own potential to love and care, and to be excited about new types of people and their qualities.

In new relationships, we tend to focus on how a person looks, because we don't know very much about them; we're trying to connect to them in a romantic way. Being physically attracted to someone is the first door we must open. But that door will lead nowhere without the ability to care for and be attracted to other traits that also make up your partner.

One day we hope to hear the "Marks" of the world say, "I never knew that I could be so turned on by a woman's intelligence and sense of love for her family, but I am. I guess I have been focusing too much on looks. Once I admitted to myself that I wanted and needed these traits in a permanent partner, I began to get as excited about them as I used to get over long blonde hair."

On the day we hear this from our "Mark," we'll be joyous for him and for the woman who becomes his wife. We will also start planning his counseling termination date.

HEALTHY DATING RULE #3

Focus on the "whole" person rather than particular "body parts." Care more about what is important to *your* happiness—instead of seeking others' approval.

CHAPTER FOUR

Foolish Dating Mistake # 4

YOU HAVE NO DATING SENSE OF HUMOR

You know you're not funny when:

1. people are drinking heavily by your third joke in a row.
2. you're forced to carry a laugh track with you.
3. your date asks the maitre'd for another table—in order to sit with other people.

THE HUMORLESS DATING PARTNER: ROBERT

Robert arrives to pick up Karen up for their first date. A mutual friend arranged this blind date, so there's a lot of tension around the meeting. Robert nervously rings the doorbell and Karen wonders if she should answer or run out the back way. As she opens the door, they both see that the other is nice looking, yet anxiety is high. Karen gathers her things and out they go for dinner, as planned.

But as Robert is walking from the door, he does not see the step down and he trips and falls flat on his face. Karen pauses a moment and asks, "Are you all right?" Robert says he is and then Karen says in a humorous tone, "Gee, I'm so flattered to have a nice-looking guy like you fall for me so quickly." Robert's entire mood changes for the worse and he responds with a lecture on home safety, how to mark a step properly and how polite people do not laugh at others when they're down. "After all," he says, "I could have been seriously injured and have required physical therapy."

Robert...lighten up!

The fall was much more embarrassing than dangerous, but he went with humiliation instead of enjoyment at Karen's wonderful ice-breaking compliment, her light way out of a sticky situation.

Let's say that you and your date have dinner reservations at 7:00 p.m. at a great restaurant that's difficult to get into. The time is 6:55 p.m. and you're stuck on the freeway in terrible traffic. The conversation could go two ways depending on whether you have decided to be an easy-humor person or a serious, uptight date:

OPTION #1–YOU LOST YOUR HUMOR AND DON'T HAVE A MAP

"Damn! I thought we left with plenty of time to get there. These reservations were nearly impossible to get and now I owe a favor to the guy who got them and we won't even be there to enjoy it. I cannot believe that these people do not know how to drive. They are all so stupid. Los Angeles is just getting worse and worse and I don't even know why I live here. Between the crime and the traffic and let's not forget the earthquakes..."

OPTION #2–FOUND THE MAP

"O.K. so here we are on the very romantic 101 Freeway stuck in intense traffic. Yes, I told you we were having dinner at a hard-to-get-into restaurant but, really, we're having an urban picnic. Boy, I really can't believe that we're all dressed up with somewhere to go but no way to get there. I was sure that we left in plenty of time, but I guess that good old Los Angeles traffic had a different date in mind. Since my well-designed plans are not looking so good right now, would you like to think of a way to save this date and pick a restaurant that you love so we can go there, instead?"

Option #1 obviously represents a person who is inflexible and takes things really hard. This attitude is almost impossible to deal with, especially with a new date. With such humorless behavior, you will have guaranteed that the date can go nowhere but up in flames. The mood is now dark, gloomy and more tense than ever.

Option #2, however, leaves lots of room for the date to tease back and say something like, "Well, this freeway is actually my dream date. Here we are alone with no phone, fax or TV. I love it out here." The date can only go up from there. Even if you are not a naturally easygoing person, tense moments present opportunities for you to practice being flexible and to see the funny side of the issue.

FOUR BASIC REASONS WHY PEOPLE HAVE NO SENSE OF HUMOR

1. Your family was not funny; they took themselves and life too seriously.
2. Your family was too funny; they took nothing about life very seriously.
3. You use seriousness as a defense, so that you will not be open for a connection.
4. You are feeling desperate to be with someone and can't find anything light about this search.

YOUR FAMILY WASN'T FUNNY

If the family to which you were born had little sense of humor, it is likely (though not certain), that they would raise a child who isn't so lighthearted, either. There are many reasons why people do not have a sense of humor. For example, some people came out of the Depression with their sense of humor intact and some have had a gray film over their lives ever since.

Negative life events, if damaging enough, can alter a person's ability to see the light side of a situation. Many people, for example, who are Holocaust survivors or second generation children of survivors, can tell you that their entire family structure had a dullness to it—as if the spark of life was taken from them. Some children grow up in a house where a single life event, such as the death of a parent, changed the course of family humor. Most people are able to return to a pre-grieving state, but not everyone. It could be that the death of a parent hurled a family into sudden poverty, which destroyed the family's spirit. Yet other families, who have had *everything* happen to them, still manage to survive with optimism—and even humor.

Again, we emphasize that it is not necessary, nor preferable, to be a joke-telling, laugh-a- minute, knee-slapping, circus clown on a date. Either way, you are difficult to be around. We are talking about the type of humor that allows you to:

1. see the light side of a situation

2. not take yourself too seriously

3. be flexible

SEEING THE LIGHT SIDE

Seeing the light side of a situation can be learned, even if you come from a gloomy, overreactive or dramatic family. Become aware of how your family usually reacts to situations and decide that such reactions are usually too strong for you. Explore alternative responses. Not everyone reacts similarly to a given situation. Some have the fabulous ability to view a problem with logic and reason, factor their feelings in as well, get help if they can't face it alone and then react accordingly.

You might come from a family that, when exposed to the same situation, reacts instead by panicking first, then overlooking and turning away from resources and reasoning and, finally, causing a huge drama in which they are quick to find and exacerbate all the negatives to the most dramatic degree. Even if this is a familiar way for you to react, it's not healthy.

Strengthen your awareness about your pessimism and try out more positive, optimistic ways of interacting. At first, you will feel as if you are faking it, but you will get more comfortable with "lightening up" as you practice.

YOU TAKE YOURSELF TOO SERIOUSLY

Taking yourself too seriously is a very difficult trait for others to be around. You have a difficult, if not impossible, time laughing at yourself and always seem to be on guard to make sure no one is laughing at you, teasing you, criticizing or taking advantage of you. Since all this scanning takes up a great deal of time in relationships, you do not have a lot left over for intimacy. Here are a couple of basic hints to remember if you tend to be this way:

1. Any talk behind your back is none of your business.

2. Assume that teasing and joking about you is playful unless told otherwise.

3. There is a difference between playful teasing and being disrespectful. (Try not to overreact...think about the teasing, and maybe get a second opinion on whether the teaser is doing it in the spirit of light fun or of rudeness.)

4. If you burden yourself with feelings of grandeur (i.e., I am much smarter than most people. I do not make stupid mistakes like that, etc.), then you are likely to take yourself way too seriously. Feeling more or less average is a gift, while feeling full of yourself and superior can be burdensome.

Once again, we recommend becoming aware of your reactions. When you are being teased, stop and think before you react. If you are unsure in the beginning whether there is malice involved (and there usually isn't), then say in a friendly tone of voice, "Boy, I sure hope you're joking." If the person doesn't respond with, "Yes, of course I am" then you can say lightly, "Well, tell me if you are or should my feelings be hurt?" Most anyone who is joking will reassure you at this point —then you need to drop it and move on. If the teasing is constant, then maybe they have a problem and you should ask them to slow down the teasing.

EXAMPLE #1–THE HARD WAY

Joan: What a nice dog you have. They say that dogs and owners begin to look alike after awhile. Yes, I'd say that's true in your case.

Bill: I don't appreciate that you're calling me a dog. Many women think I'm good-looking. And what about you? You have make-up like a circus clown and are built like the fat lady.

Oh, poor Bill.

EXAMPLE #2–THE EASIER WAY

Choice A—Be Funny Back

Bill: Oh really? Well if you keep talking like that, I may have to give you a little bite!

Choice B—It Hurt You

But you are still willing to use some light humor to let her know:

Bill: Thank you very much! Tell me that you're joking or I might have to develop some hurt feelings here.

Joan: Oh, I'm sorry. No, I was just joking.

Being flexible in these situations means having more than one option for how to respond when you feel bad. People who are not easily humiliated do have an easier life. They are more easygoing in relationships. If shame and humiliation prevailed in your childhood home, however, you may be sensitized to these things and, as a result, much of what you experience now is viewed from that earlier, traumatic context.

You do not have to be stuck in this place. Everyone can learn to differentiate between teasing and put-downs, and everyone can learn different ways to react to what feel like threats. The most seriously inflexible people seem to be challenged the most by others to be flexible. This is definitely a quality that can be developed with time, practice and, as usual, awareness.

YOUR FAMILY WAS TOO FUNNY

Now *this* is not funny. The "chuckle-a-minute" family can raise some pretty serious kids. We are not talking about the family with a great sense of humor that is in balance with the serious things. We are discussing the family type that takes nothing seriously, leaving a huge imbalance in the family structure. This can cause the children, when very young, to begin acting like serious adults.

Example:

Mom: I can't believe that the mortgage company has no sense of humor. I told them we were having a bad hair month and couldn't pay them and now they are all cranky.

Scott (14-year-old):
        You didn't pay the house payment? Will something happen?

Mom: Oh, yeah. We'll get enough threatening letters from them to build a bonfire in the backyard. I'll get some marshmallows and sticks and we'll have a family cookout on them!

Scott: Could we lose the house?

Mom: Well we won't 'lose' it. It will always be here on Elm Street.

Poor Scott is thrown into total insecurity because Mom cannot stop being funny long enough to realize that if she and her husband are always "having a good time" and taking nothing seriously, they are likely to create children who worry for them. It's a very hard habit to break when they grow up and begin to have adult relationships. It feels like disaster could always be around the corner and that it is up to them to handle everything. Humor appears to them to be the root of all evil.

THE GOOFY FAMILY

Another type of "too-funny-for-words" family is the "goofy" family. These are the kind of people who make a dumb joke every chance they get. They are not beyond a pun for every occasion and tell so many bad jokes that you are afraid to bring your friends home to meet them. Polite friends will say that your parents are "cute." The truth is that they hide behind this bad standup comedian mask and rarely come out. It is difficult to count on people like this. They will humiliate you in front of others and annoy you when you are alone with them. It is a hard situation because they are probably not mean-spirited. They genuinely feel that they are funny and that others are way too serious and not living life to its fullest. The feeling is that their children are lucky to have fun parents. Unfortunately for those of us with parents like this, well-meaning rather than funny as they may be, they are viewed by others as embarrassing. Their grown children may have a poor understanding of what humor is and, as a result, want nothing to do with it.

Example 1:

Dad: Oh, it sure is good to meet a friend of Sally's...cause we didn't think she had any. Ha! Ha! Ha!

Sally: (trying to control the situation)
Dad, Adam is at M.I.T. studying computer science.

Dad: Wow, M.I.T. Does that stand for More Intense Technobabble?

Sally: Dad, please. Adam is an honor student and is doing very well and takes his education very seriously.

Mom: Yes, dear. Honor is a serious matter. Knock, knock. Who's there? Honor, Honor who? Honor you. (Ha, Ha, Ha!) Gonna ask me what's for dinner?

Sally: (embarrassed and humiliated.)
Adam, we have to go now.

Maybe you want Sally's parents to be arrested by the humor police but they are how they are. It's difficult to explain to parents the ways in which they accidentally hurt you. Another example indicates how Sally could deflect responsibility for her parents and use a little humor of her own.

Example 2:

Dad: Oh, it sure is good to meet a friend of Sally's...cause we didn't think she had any. Ha! Ha! Ha!

Sally: (trying to control the situation.)
Dad, Adam is at M.I.T. studying computer science.

Dad: Wow, M.I.T. Does that stand for More Intense Technobabble?

Sally: (she could decide not to respond at all, or come back with the following kind of retort)
Gee Dad, dumb M.I.T. joke. Anyway, Adam is an honor student and is doing very well and takes his education very seriously.

Mom: Yes, dear. Honor is a serious matter. Knock, knock. Who's there? Honor, Honor who? (Ha! Ha! Ha!) Gonna ask me what's for dinner?

Sally: (with a light tone)
Knock, knock. Who's there? Not us if you keep up this joke-a-thon!

Sally could show Adam around the house and when alone tell him that her parents mean well and every once in awhile they get out a *good* joke! It's up to Adam to not be a judgmental person and see the light side of the situation.

YOU USE SERIOUSNESS AS A DEFENSE SO YOU WON'T BE OPEN FOR A CONNECTION

All of us would like to think that we are ready for healthy relationships. We may even appear to be doing everything possible to be available for the right mate. However, no matter how ready we feel to engage in this partnership, we may simultaneously be fearful. It's scary to get involved and get intimate with someone. The risks can get pretty high and we may get hurt. *A great deal of courage is required to be happy.* Many people hate being unhappy, but at least they are accustomed to it and there are few risks in that stagnant place. *Happiness requires that we stay optimistic in the face of emotional terror.*

By being open, you risk:

the possibility that the other person might be lying to you

disappointment after feeling hopeful

abandonment or rejection

feeling more empty then before you got involved

It is easy to understand why we would want to put up huge defenses. These defenses, however, block humor and create a wall between you and others so that even though you are acting close, the defenses are in the way.

Example: Defenses At Work

Sarah: This weekend is our three-month dating anniversary, Doug. I'm having a great time with you.

Doug: Me, too. Would you like to do something special on Saturday to celebrate?

Sarah: Definitely! How about going to Chez Monique? (teasingly) It's a really fine restaurant and, as you know, I am only interested in your money.

Doug: That's not funny, Sarah, but I'll take you there if you want to go.

Sarah: O.K., that's great.
(Again with a twinkle in her eye)
And let's take your BMW. You know that car made me love you, Doug.

Doug: Oh, you love me for my car?

Sarah: (Laughingly)
         Well I love you more than my new Honda, but a little less
         than your BMW.

Doug: (Flips out and is very angry with Sarah and cancels the whole
         weekend because he feels she is money-hungry and
         unappreciative.)

If Doug had taken the time to remind himself of how caring
Sarah has been so far, with no indication of shallowness regarding
money, he'd have realized that Sarah:

1. makes great money on her own.

2. is completely self-supporting and in good control of her
   money.

3. was raised to count only on herself financially and if she
   ever married someone who also made a good living, that
   would be icing on the cake.

4. feels so secure financially that she thought it was funny to
   tease Doug about money and materialism, since it is so
   clear to her that she is not out for anyone's money nor is
   she materialistic.

But Doug is afraid of intimacy and is defended against a close
connection with Sarah, as is evident by his deficient sense of
humor. Sarah was only joking around and did not know that Doug:

1. has Depression-era parents who have passed down their
   fear of not having enough money.

2. has struggled for every penny in order to go to law
   school.

3. worries that somehow he will lose what he has (as his
   parents did) or someone will trick him out of it.

4. desires *very* much to trust someone and share his future
   wealth and is working on that goal.

Sarah could have joked with more sensitivity had she known,
and Doug could have taken a risk and gone with the teasing:

Sarah: This weekend is our six-month dating anniversary, Doug. I
         care about you a lot.

Doug: I care for you, too, Sarah. Let's go out on the town and
         celebrate a great six months.

Sarah: Definitely! How about going to Chez Monique?" (Teasingly) "It's a really nice restaurant if you would be willing to spend the big bucks on me. You know that besides your good looks, intelligence, generosity, thoughtfulness and charm, that I'm only after your money!

Doug: Oh really? (Teasingly, back) Then perhaps we can go to Chez Jacques In The Box for dinner if that's how you feel.

Sarah: O.K., fine, but can we take your BMW so that I will have some dignity left?

Doug: All right then, I'll take you in the BMW and I am not even going to tell you where. You'll have to take your chances with me on Saturday night—deal?

Sarah: Great! It's a deal!

Conversation #2 had a lot more security to it. Defenses were not up and humor was allowed to flourish. It really does take the ability to relax a little and not anticipate trouble in order for your sense of humor to be revealed. These are not world-peace negotiations. This is dating. You're supposed to have a good time. The only decisions you should be making in the beginning stage are what to wear, where to go and whether you want one more date after this one. That is it!

Stop pressuring yourself to make life-changing decisions within the first few months of seeing someone. Let your defenses come down a little and your sense of humor come out. Humor is absolutely one of the best ways for people to connect. It is usually a tension breaker and it's fun and attractive. If you find that you are not connecting with people initially or that you lose your connection later down the line, check your humor. Is it still there?

DESPERATION SHOOTS HUMOR INTO A MILLION PIECES

The search for someone compatible and special can be a long one. At times, it can feel like your second, full-time job. And the reality is that if you are truly serious about finding the right someone for you, many hours of creative thinking and follow-through are involved. We believe that the days of marrying someone you knew in high school are about over. A lot of us aren't marrying until our late thirties or are marrying for the second time later on. Even the "college sweetheart" idea is becoming a part of the past.

Meeting people is becoming more and more difficult. It's not unusual for people to get up in the morning, go to work, speak to very few people all day and then get home late and go to bed. On the weekends, busy people run errands, do laundry, get extra work done and, if they're lucky, get some exercise or go out and have fun. People frequently communicate more by e-mail than by phone. In-person interaction is diminishing and a single person in search of a partner is increasingly forced to be creative and assertive. Singles are placing ads, attending singles-only events, hiring matchmakers, testing computer or video dating, using the Internet and filling the bookstores and coffee houses. We are in search of ways to meet people.

In our seminars, we are constantly asking people to put more time into their love life. This makes people want to throw things at us and have us dragged from the front of the room. Yes, we are all time-stressed. Adding one more "chore" might cause you to go over the stress edge. However, we always ask people to stop a moment and figure out how many hours a week they put into ensuring their career success. Add up all the hours at work and all that you spend away from work to ensure success and reach your goals. For most people, the total is between thirty-five and seventy-five hours each week. When asked how many hours they put into reaching their relationship goals, it's more like between zero and two hours. Positive results follow our focus. Obviously, it's not necessary to put in a forty-hour week in search of Mr., Ms. or Dr. Right. But we do have to do *something* and it can be tiring, scary and hard.

THE DREADED, DESPERATE FEELING ARRIVES

As time goes on and years and years of dating go by, we can begin to feel desperate to find someone and begin a new life as a couple. This is completely understandable. It is also not unusual to lose one's sense of humor in this search that gets old fast. Unfortunately, the loss of your humor makes the wait completely unbearable. With no way to laugh at the situation, you begin to be tense and push others to "not waste your time." You see hidden meaning in everything and try to judge others quickly so that you do not once again invest in someone who's not going to work out. You are a *drag*!

You could be out on a date with Mr./Ms. Jay Leno/Rosie O'Donnell and not find a single light moment because you are so stressed about dating in general. Jay/Rosie isn't going to know that you're a terrific person—except for the many disappointments that have left you a little down right now. He/she will think you're a bore. How do you keep it fresh? How do you go out each weekend on yet another date and tell the same stories repeatedly, ask the same dumb questions and not throw food across the room? Perhaps the following suggestions will help you stay sane, as opposed to feeling desperate:

1. *Try to find things that are fun for you to do and that will also allow you to meet people.*

Do something different. Get out there and have fun and if you meet someone, it's a bonus. Sign up for group tennis lessons, French lessons, classes at adult schools, dance lessons, canoeing, white-water rafting trips, sailing clubs, running clubs, lectures, etc. Anything that would be an adventure for you will put you in a good mood as a start, but also reenergize your week. Challenge yourself to get out there and try something new. Then, either way, you'll win.

Tami was a nurse who forever complained that there were "no good single men out there" and she felt completely hopeless about finding someone. To get away from the depressing dating cycle she was in, we suggested she think of something she would like to do but thought was too stupid, too expensive or too time-consuming. After much thought, she shyly admitted to a desire to act. Upon further gentle questioning, we found that she wanted to do comedy. Her job could be difficult and depressing and she envied people who laughed for a living. We encouraged her to sign up for an improv class, even though she had many reasons (better known as excuses) not to.

Tami let us know later that the first class was a bomb because she didn't like the teacher and couldn't bring herself to get up in front of class. However, a second class proved to be quite successful. She tried out a class assignment that led to dating her class partner.

2. *Try to keep first dates short.*

Meeting for a cup of coffee is a great way to avoid investing too much time, money and energy in a first or second meeting. Otherwise, if we invest a great deal, we can suffer a bigger disappointment if it doesn't work out at all. It is definitely easier to shake off a thirty-minute cup of coffee than a ten-hour day trip with someone who turns out to be absolutely not for you.

THE DATE FROM HELL CAN DAMPEN YOUR HUMOR

After spending all day at the races and dinner with Suzanne, Craig was ready to check himself into the funny farm. Suzanne talked nonstop. From the moment he picked her up until the second he dropped her off she gabbed about people he didn't know and a thousand other things he couldn't even remember.

At one period during the date, Craig timed Suzanne and found that she spoke in a monologue for forty-five minutes, without even checking to see if he was still standing there. After forty-five minutes, she glanced over to confirm his presence—but then continued talking about her Uncle Mel's farm in Iowa.

Craig was so shaken at the end of eight hours that he was actually vibrating; he vowed never to go on a date again. Had Craig made only a coffee date with Suzanne, she'd have only been able to monopolize his time for thirty minutes before he'd have realized the problem and ended the date.

3. *Take small breaks from dating when necessary.*

Even though we tell you to persevere when it comes to your romantic life, you may need some small breaks from this job, too. If you find that your sense of humor is drooping and you can't seem to get psyched up for a date, it may be time for a little break. Take two to three weeks off without even thinking about dating and get some rest from it.

Maybe you need to get out of town or plan some time alone or with family and friends to regain your dating stamina. We all need to get away from pursuing our goals from time to time. We can't expect to draw on our emotional bank account over and over again without ever depositing anything in it. After getting away for awhile and not putting energy into dating, you can return to the dating scene rejuvenated.

4. *Write out your feelings of frustration, loneliness or impatience in a journal.*

Sometimes dating accentuates our desire to become part of a couple—and it can hurt. Getting the feelings out by talking to friends or keeping a journal are fabulous ways to avoid getting stuck in the feelings. This helps you find the strength to keep going.

You can write a few words about disastrous dates or you can write volumes. Writing is a great release. A man who attended one of our seminars described how he kept a "nightmare date log" just to amuse his friends. In that way, all bad dates got entered in the log, his friends got a kick out of his experiences and he kept his sense of humor about the dating process. Remember that everyone can be either a dream date or a nightmare date, depending on the point-of-view of the other person. So it is not about making fun of the other person. It's about having fun with what didn't work for you instead of getting depressed.

TURN A NIGHTMARE INTO A DREAM STORY

Here's an example of a nightmare date to laugh at later:

Lily was excited when Harris asked her out. She thought he was handsome, smart and funny. She put effort into looking great and they had a fabulous time dining in an al fresco restaurant overlooking the lights of the city. When Harris kissed her lightly, Lily felt thrilled. The date was great and they shared coffee at Lily's home after talking until 2:00 a.m.

Upon leaving, Harris mentioned to Lily that she was everything he hoped she would be. Lily was melting. Then Harris let her know that he now felt more sure than ever that she would be the perfect girl for his brother.

Lily was in too much shock to speak as he went on to say that his brother was not a good judge of character and that he was helping him find a great girl. Harris was in shock when Lily threw him out and refused his phone calls.

Lily decided that this was a great story to tell over and over; people were amazed to hear it. She turned a negative into a positive by applying the lighter side to a weird situation. Humor is a dating lifesaver, so keep it close by and use it when necessary.

IF YOUR HUMOR WELL FEELS A LITTLE DRY:

◊   Observe funny people you know and emulate them.

◊   Take classes on humor or acting.

◊   Read or watch comedies.

◊   Ask about funny stories on dates (i.e., "What was the funniest thing you and your brothers ever did together?")

SUMMARY

It is a difficult to maintain humor when dating feels so serious, yet can be a life saver, for both yourself and others. Seeing the funny side lowers your blood pressure as well as your dating pressure.

HEALTHY DATING RULE #4

Practice searching for the lighter, funnier side of things. Don't take everything so personally.

CHAPTER FIVE

Foolish Dating Mistake #5

YOUR NEGATIVE
HABITS & ATTITUDES
BLOCK COMMITMENT

QUIZ:

You believe:

1. good hygiene is optional.
2. drinking six cocktails before the appetizer is O.K.
3. discussing the state of your digestive system passes for romantic dinner conversation.

This is a "look-at-yourself-in-a-mirror" chapter to try to discover what your negative traits are and how they're affecting your dating relationships. It's very easy to find the flaws in others and not see them in ourselves. Everyone has negative traits and behaviors, but it is much worse if you have no idea what they are and when yours are obvious and active. This means you'll never improve yourself or be aware of how your traits and behaviors affect your ability to date successfully. The following is a list of seven negative habits and attitudes that are sure to extinguish the fire of any great date:

1. being too critical
2. being inflexible
3. using drugs or abusing alcohol

4. being sloppy or dirty

5. being moody

6. being uncreative and lazy

7. disrespecting your date

#1—BEING TOO CRITICAL—
Or A Date With You Makes Me Feel Like Having Plastic Surgery

Critical people do not usually realize that they criticize others. Mostly they think of themselves as honest or helpful. But the truth is that critical individuals tear away at the fiber of people's self-esteem. If the critical man finds himself on a date with someone who has good self-esteem, he will be dumped immediately. People with high esteem do not criticize others and do not tolerate having it imposed on them.

Example:

Tom: (picking up Margie for a date)
        Hi. You look good! But are you really going to wear *that* coat? The restaurant we're going to is a bit dressy.

Margie: This is the only coat I have. I think it's pretty nice. I'm sure it will be O.K.

Tom: (at the restaurant)
        Tell me you're not going to order the pasta again. This place is well-known for its seafood. At least get a seafood pasta.

Margie: I love spaghetti bolognese, Tom. I just had seafood last night.

Tom: (smiling)
        You are risking becoming a bore, Margie! Ha! Ha!

Margie: (inner thought)
        And you are risking never seeing me again, you creep!

Margie does not let the fact that Tom is teasing, suggesting, joking, commenting, etc. take her away from the more important fact that Tom was critical. In between these "reviews" he was charming and fun to be with; however, people with good feelings about themselves are sensitive to those who have a nasty streak—no matter how covert it is.

One accidentally offensive comment does not a critical person make. Rather, critical people are more likely to present their criticism as a generalized point-of-view that suffuses the content of the entire date conversation.

When critical people date those with low self-esteem, they bring out the worst in each other. They bring out the worst in each other. Such a relationship is guaranteed to produce unhappiness.

Example:

Kevin: (picks up Kelly and is overwhelmed by how beautiful she is) Hi, you look incredible!"

Kelly: Well what does 'incredible' mean?

Kevin: That you look so pretty.

Kelly: Well, that doesn't really give me any information. Do you like my hair or my dress or what?

Kevin: It's all so great.

Kelly: Thanks. We better get going or we'll be late as usual.

Kevin: (who feels bad that he didn't get there a few minutes earlier so that they would have time to talk) Listen, I'm sorry that I didn't have time today to wash the car. I washed it a few days ago and I meant to today, but it's tax season and I worked fourteen hours today.

Kelly: We all have our priorities.

Kevin: So what movie would you like to see?

Kelly: I thought maybe a comedy might be nice. I checked the times and there's one playing right by the restaurant at a really good time. What do you think?

Kevin: (feeling desperate that he didn't take care of making plans) O.K. great. And isn't there that little boutique open late right next to it? Maybe you'll see something you like there and I could buy you a present.

Stop! These kinds of couples actually think that they get along well. Since Kevin does not appreciate himself at all, he will not notice that he is being picked on. Kelly probably feels that Kevin needs her assistance in dressing better, communicating more accurately and being a better person in general. So the dance begins, but it usually ends with a totally devastated Kevin and an angry and frustrated Kelly.

Critical behavior is a form of control over others. It makes you the authority figure. It also keeps the focus off your real or imagined flaws.

Before you write this section off as "not about me," think twice and ask some friends if they experience this critical attitude in you. This new knowledge about your behavior, if true, could change your dating situation for the positive in a big way.

#2–BEING INFLEXIBLE–
Or It's My Way Or The Highway

Getting to know someone definitely requires flexibility. Unfortunately, when we are nervous or vulnerable (as we tend to feel when first dating someone), we may try to stick to certain rules, plans, attitudes or opinions that make us feel safe. This is better known as being inflexible. This is a sure relationship killer because it makes your date feel invisible, unimportant, unheard and inferior. It makes you look argumentative, unspontaneous, anxious, hard to get along with and stuck.

WHY PEOPLE ARE INFLEXIBLE

People who are inflexible are usually scared. They are afraid of:

1. being exposed as a fake
2. not measuring up
3. losing control
4. losing someone or something
5 looking inferior

For many people it is very frightening to be spontaneous and try new things—or try old things in new ways. It takes courage to travel to a new destination without a compass. Some even liken the feeling to walking a tightrope without a net. Inflexibility feels safe because with it comes a used, worn, tried-and-true road map. You do things the way you have done them a million times before. It feels familiar even if it isn't healthy, fun or new.

Example:

INFLEXIBLE DATE DIALOGUE

Frank: There is this great little playhouse near the airport that always has something good going on. I hope we can get there by 8:00 p.m.

Allison: I know a great shortcut near the airport that can save us some time. Turn right at the next light.

Frank: Thanks, Allison, but I always take the 405 Freeway and then Century Boulevard to get to the airport area.

Allison: But I'm really sure of this way and if you're concerned about time, I know it will help.

Frank: Thanks. This is the best way.

Allison: (near the playhouse) Oh, Mark, I saw a parking space right in front of the theater. We could probably get it if we turn in here.

Frank: No, I never park in front. The neighborhood isn't safe so I park in the lot.

Allison: But the space is right in front of the box office and they have someone there the whole time.

Frank: I've never done that. I always park in that pay lot over there and nothing has ever gone wrong.

Who wants to tell Frank where to park it? If the evening continues to be about how he always does things and his beliefs that are written in stone, then there is not a lot of room for Allison in the relationship.

INFLEXIBLE DATE SCENARIO NO. 2 –
OR MY TASTES ARE FIXED, FOREVER

We like to share the story of Judy, who constantly was amazed by Gary's inability to change anything from the way it was originally done or planned. The final straw was on Valentine's Day when Judy went out of her way to make a gorgeous package for Gary, filled with men's underwear in great colors. She had stripes and bold colors and some were even sexy string bikinis. Judy thought the package was fun and provocative and enjoyable for them both. However, when Gary opened the present, he was insulted. As he informed her, "If white briefs were good enough for my Dad to wear all of his life, then they're good enough for me to wear all of mine."

Perhaps Gary could have just put the underwear on for a few minutes and been playful with it. And perhaps Mark could have tried Allison's alternative route for getting to the play. These are small things to be inflexible about. Yet it is likely that if your new date is so closed on the small stuff, then his or her stance on the big stuff is even more rigid.

#3—USING DRUGS OR ABUSING ALCOHOL

Or I'm Sure The Date Was Great IF I Could Only Remember It Or...I Could Stop Drinking Anytime, It's No Problem

This section is not for those who travel in a drug or alcohol "circle." If everyone you know gets high and you prefer to date those who do, skip this part and proceed immediately to a Twelve-Step Program.

If you wish to be in a healthy relationship, however, the drugs and alcohol cannot be a major aspect of what you do, whether together or apart. When the students in our seminars are asked how many drinks they consider normal for an entire evening out, the major consensus is zero to two drinks. People are just not tolerating the drinking and drugging of the past. We want to know who the person really is without a buzz. We know that a drink might help to take off "the edge" before or during a date, but it would serve you better to show up nervous.

Most people who claim they are better to be around after a drink or two do not have a realistic perception of themselves. If you absolutely have to use something before a date to get through it, your problem isn't dating, it's alcohol and drug use. Get help.

Please stop telling yourself that people don't care how much you drink or how high you get on a date and that if they do they are just uptight. It is difficult to get a second date with healthy people when you are high on a date. No matter how relaxed or in control you think you look, to a person without an addiction, you look "out of it" and they will want "out of" a date with you as fast as they can.

#4–BEING SLOPPY OR DIRTY

Or Yuck! The Basics of Hygiene Are A Must

We know that this section must seem obvious, but based on the people we see who complain about it, it is not. Naturally, one should do the bare minimum before a date. A shower is mandatory, along with shaving and applying deodorant. Clean clothing and freshly brushed teeth are the sine qua non of those who expect to go the dating distance with anyone.

THOSE EXTRA AESTHETIC EFFORTS GO A LONG WAY

Your Body

Beyond the obvious minimum for a date is the use of perfume or cologne. But be subtle. This is a detail that often goes overlooked, but which can make it difficult for your date to be in close proximity to you if your scent is too strong. Your aroma should not linger in a room longer than you do, no matter how wonderful the scent. Buy only high quality perfume or cologne and use it sparingly.

The following dating suggestions may seem over-the-top in their apparent obviousness and, yet, our clinical experience indicates otherwise. Here goes:

Avoid disgusting noises, but apologize immediately if you commit such a faux pas.

Pay attention to how you eat. You need not be the Queen of England, but do curb your tendencies toward gluttonous eating. Eat slowly, do not eat off the plates of others, keep your mouth closed while chewing and do not slurp anything.

Remember what your mother told you about covering your mouth when you yawn or cough and never, ever, ever, pick at any part of your body while on a date!

A MESSY ENVIRONMENT CAN MESS THINGS UP FOR ROMANCE

The last item to be considered before you date is the sloppiness or condition of your car or home if your date will be in either one. There is no explaining away filth, so be honest with yourself about your surroundings. If you want to get a second date, *get a sponge.* Never put yourself in the position of needing to continuously apologize to someone you hardly know. They'll think the worst if you have to push aside uneaten french fries and smelly sweats to make it possible for them to sit in your car. Take time and care to put your auto and home in order. Perfection should never be a requirement but a presentable appearance is a must. When dates are afraid to use your bathroom, it puts you in a negative light—even if you are a great person.

#5—BEING MOODY

Or I Always Wanted To Date A Doctor But Not Dr. Jeckyl & Mr. Hyde

There are three kinds of moody behavior:

1. The kind that is a mood disorder, requiring treatment and possibly medication.
2. The kind that results from jealousy and possessiveness.
3. The kind that we shall discuss, which is that of "moodiness" of character. This type of moodiness is within the person's control. Forget the excuses. If you do not have a clinical disorder, you are just difficult to be around. To excuse yourself, perhaps you say one or more of the following:

THE TOP 10 LIST OF EXCUSES WHY I AM MOODY AND I DON'T WANT TO CHANGE

10. I am just an intense person.
9. So what if I'm not always Chuckles the Clown!
8. I have a lot on my mind.
7. I have a lot of responsibilities.
6. I get more attention when I'm down or grouchy.
5. It's a tough world out there.
4. It's in my genes.
3. I'm just tired.
2. I'm too old to change.
1. People should accept me as I am.

We are not required to always be in a good mood to have a successful dating (or life) experience. You should, however, be able to show up in a pretty good mood in the initial and beginning phases of dating because you are not yet close enough to the person to confide in him or her the reason for a particularly bad mood. It is foolish to show up on a second date in a terrible mood and say that you are not usually like this and expect your date to understand.

If your moods flip-flop at a moment's notice, it is vital to understand what or who sets you off. No one who's healthy wants to go on a roller-coaster ride with your emotions. It is tiring and frustrating to date someone who starts out in a good mood and ends up in the pits, or someone who shows up in a bad mood and needs you to put on tap shoes and entertain them until they're happy. It is just too much trouble.

WHY DO WE GET MOODY?

Moodiness is the character trait of an immature person. Naturally, we're not talking about the occasional bad hour or day that we all have. We're talking about moodiness as a behavior pattern, which causes others to feel as if they can't count on you to be a steady individual. When in your company they feel off-balance and uneasy wondering when you will fall into a funk. When trying to figure out your own moody behavior, notice that it is an attention-getter (albeit negative attention) and tends to control the moods of others. If everyone is in an O.K. mood while out to dinner and you show up carrying your "wet blanket," realize that the whole mood of the evening will likely be altered for the worse. You need to take a look at what your payoff is for these bad moods (i.e., attention, feeling of control) and compare it to what you are losing (i.e., the ability to date anyone great).

Moodiness can also result from being possessive and jealous. We can become this way as a result of low self-esteem or past hurts. If you tend to be like this in relationships, you may be causing the beginning of the end. You can and must change these attitudes.

HOW TO STOP YOUR MOODINESS

When you are ready to stop torturing others with your moody behavior, you will focus on:

1. positive things before a date begins
2. getting enough food
3. rest

It is important to identify the things that set you off (the trigger points). You owe it to yourself and others to be a positive person who is pleasant to be with most of the time. We all have our highs and lows, and that is normal. But you must stop blaming others for *your* bad moods; it is not their fault. It's you, and only you can find out what you need in order to feel better.

#6—YOU ARE UNCREATIVE & LAZY

Or Could You Pass The Remote Control?

Bet on this being a short section because it's the easiest to cure. Write down any twenty dates that you have planned and tell us if you start falling asleep with the pen in your hand? Dinner, movie or rental video are fun options, but should not be the only choices on the menu. Many people worry about investing too much time or effort into making a date great because they may not like the person. That is an unproductive attitude. It is better to think about it like this: *"Even if this person turns out to be wrong for me, at least the date itself might be fun."*

HOW TO IMPROVE YOUR DATING CREATIVITY

Perhaps planning something wonderful that you have always wanted to do will make the date a better experience by bringing out the best in both of you. At the very least, you can feel good that you were creative and put forth some effort. Remember that "creative" does not necessarily mean "expensive." Some of the least expensive dates can be the most interesting and memorable. Friends can be a great resource for dating ideas. Look through your local town paper for ideas. How about taking a cooking seminar together for a couple of hours or checking out your local nature walks? A small blanket and picnic basket works wonders if your date is stuck in an office forty hours a week.

Think of what tourists do when they come to your town. Think of something you have always wanted to do but would be bad at (such as ice skating) and bring your sense of humor. Try the circus (as in taking a date, not running away with). Dates do not have to be "knock-your-socks-off" types of events. We are only asking you not to fall into too much of a rut—for your own sake. Dating can get boring and tiresome. Have some fun.

#7–DISRESPECTING YOUR DATE

Or Excuse Me!

This category is sometimes subtle, but still deadly. It is a lot of little foolish mistakes rolled into one. If you have no clue as to why dating is not going well for you, this may be the information you need. These are behaviors that make your date feel bad and not want to see you again.

DISRESPECTFUL BEHAVIORS THAT CAN END A RELATIONSHIP

The following are examples of behaviors that can get you dumped before you know what hit you:

1. bad language
2. ignoring your date
3. flirting with others
4. giving unusual amounts of attention to food servers
5. tardiness
6. inappropriate phone calling hours or drop-in visits
7. canceling without notice
8. making fun of or inappropriate teasing
9. comments that are too personal
10. walking way ahead
11. honking the horn for pickup
12. dropping your date off at the curb with the motor running
13. jumping out of the car with the motor running

14. ordering huge amounts of expensive food (when you are
not paying); and other rude behavior

SHOW RESPECT TO YOUR DATE, NO MATTER WHAT

We are sure that you get the general idea here, but a few details
are worth mentioning. Whether or not you decide that you like or are
attracted to your date, he or she deserves your respect and vice-
versa. Do not use offensive language. Learn to express anger or
humor without getting hostile or profane. When calling another
person, keep the calls between 9:00 a.m. (maybe even later on
Sundays or holidays) and 9:00 p.m., unless told otherwise.
Avoiding the dinner hour (around 6:30 to 7:30 p.m.). Always call
before visiting a person's home or place of work. When cancelling a
date and unless it is a dire emergency, give a minimum two-day
notice. Other people have lives and plans they would like to make.

Please be on time or die trying! This means whether you are
driving or being picked up. When you run late, you are making a
statement that the other person's time is not valuable. Horns should
only be honked before someone in a bigger car is about to crash into
you. Don't honk for people.

It is polite to start a date off with a quick, light compliment if
you have one. "It's good to see you" will do. While on the date,
attempt to treat the person with respect and focus on him or her.
Being overly friendly to the food server or treating the server like a
servant makes a very poor impression. Flirting or degrading others
only makes you look rude or insecure.

Guess which mistake Nancy is making with Mitch:

DISRESPECTFUL TEASING

Mitch: I hope you like Italian food because this is a great restaurant.

Nancy: (Laughing and looking at Mitch's rounded tummy)
Yes, it sure looks like you get here often enough!

Mitch: I guess I haven't been working out too much lately.

Nancy: (Joking tone)
No, I guess not. There's the proof, right? The tummy tells no
lies, Mitch.

Mitch: Yeah, I guess so.

Nancy: (More seriously,)
> Have you ever tried a personal trainer? I have one and I could give you his phone number. You have such a great face and it seems like a shame.

Nancy needs to get a grip on her teasing personal comments.

SHOWING SENSITIVITY TO YOUR DATE

Be sensitive when deciding what to do on a date when the other person is paying all or part of the expense. Continue this "minimum required amount of sensitivity" when ending the date. Both people should get out of the car or walk together to each other's cars and say good-bye. Do not jump on people in a parking lot for a kiss and above all, *do not say you will call if you know you will not be calling.* Lying is rude. Here are some ways to deal with that last moment and still be polite.

Sensitive Example #1

You like him but are not sure how he feels.

At the end of the date, take a chance and say, "I had a great time and I hope you call" or "I would be glad if you called again—Good Night!"

Sensitive Example #2

You like her but are not sure how she feels.

At the end of the date, take the chance and say, "I had a great time with you and I would like to do it again if you would." If you are still unsure how she feels, call her several days later and ask her out again. If she says no, make sure she has a way to reach you, tell her again that you want to get together and to please call you as soon as she knows when she can. This takes the guesswork out of it. If she is interested and mature, she will call you back and say which day is good since you have already made the first move.

NEVER PROMISE "I'LL CALL" IF YOU KNOW YOU WON'T

Resist the "I'll-call-you" line when you do not mean it. It is perfectly O.K. to end a date by saying, "Good Night and thanks for the date" or "Thanks for going out tonight." The End! If you are the woman and he asks you out at the end of the date (or on the phone) and you are sure that you do not want to go out again, just say, "I really want to thank you for this date and I had a nice time, but I don't think we have a lot in common, so I'm going to have to say no." Thank him and be done with it. What do you think men feel when they are encouraged to call you, only to find you busy from now until Groundhog Day 2005? Don't drag it out. No one has to be the polite angel, but give some thought to doing the sensitive, respectful act whenever possible.

SUMMARY

We all have faults that push people away. We have discussed many such traits in this chapter with suggestions on how to change them. All of these traits are changeable if you accept that they are causing or contributing to the lack of success in dating. Some are problems of attitude, some are behavior problems, but all of them create negative results in relationships.

HEALTHY DATING RULE #5

Discover what your personal problems are and be open to changing them on your own or getting help to do so.

CHAPTER SIX

Foolish Dating Mistake # 6

YOU RESIST COMMITMENT

QUIZ:

You avoid commitment by…

1. asking someone out for a date ten minutes before you plan to pick them up.
2. getting rid of your dog every time it needs to be groomed.
3. signing all contracts with disappearing ink.

Fear and resistance to committing to someone can often ruin an otherwise good relationship. Healthy people want and look forward to the exclusivity, accountability and stability of a committed relationship. People who are afraid of commitment avoid it. They are only interested in the part of a relationship that is easy, self-serving and spontaneous.

Commitment Phobia: This fear of commitment is just as real and limiting as is the fear of flying. The airplane phobic refuses to fly and takes only trains and buses to destinations. The commitment phobic refuses to take that final step into an exclusive and committed relationship and, instead, chooses only short-term encounters as a poor substitute.

With commitment phobia you can have relationships, but they do not include vulnerability or plans for the future. You also get angry when expectations are placed on you, and you are stingy in order to keep your partner from thinking you are serious about them.

WHAT IS COMMITMENT ANYWAY?

There is a major difference between not wanting commitment, knowing you are not ready for commitment and resisting it because of emotional fear. A person who does not want commitment may have good reasons for not wanting it. This person may still want a relationship, but one without commitment. People may know that they are not ready for it; sometimes it's a smart decision not to commit.

In many areas of a relationship, commitment becomes a focal issue. Beyond a vow to be exclusive or to marry is the promise to take the relationship seriously. This means *to honor your word, to put time and energy into it and to develop good communication.*

Tom said he was a person who valued commitment, but when dating Lynn this did not prove to be the case. Although they both liked each other, their conversation—after six months—sounds like this:

Lynn: (on the telephone with Tom) Hi, Tom! I am really looking forward to tomorrow.

Tom: Lynn, I'm sorry but I decided that I need to stay home and take care of some personal things.

Lynn: But we had plans, and last week we had to change plans at the last minute, too.

Tom: Well, things don't always work out as we plan. I'm sorry. What more can I say?

Lynn: I thought you were more committed to this relationship.

Tom: What does changing my mind about plans have to do with commitment? I am not dating anyone else.

Lynn feels Tom is too casual with their relationship. He thinks because he is not seeing other women that he is committed. But Lynn wants respect for the momentum and intensity of the experiences they have while they are dating. She is doubting whether Tom will be an equally involved and trusting partner.

Tom is being selfish and self-centered. He breaks his word to convenience himself, but doesn't see this as a problem. He's not putting energy into the kind of dating that helps couples transcend to new levels of intimacy. He also does not communicate in a deep way. In the above scenario, he is vague, unemotional and defensive.

Lynn should boot Tom out the door. And Tom needs to acknowledge and figure out the reasons for his foolish, selfish behavior.

WHY ARE YOU SO AFRAID OF COMMITMENT?

The answer is simple: You are consumed with the *fear* that something bad will happen to you once you surrender to a relationship and become vulnerable.

A common and devastating fear is the fear of rejection. Of course, you will be rejected sometimes. We all get rejected and we all hate it. When it happens, you tell yourself, "I will never take a risk like this again; it's not worth it." After the rejection, you feel like a putz who threw away control and is left without dignity. You are so hurt by being dumped that your thinking goes out of whack.

Instead, think about this. The only truth that the rejection reveals is that someone changed his or her mind about wanting to date you.

We work with many clients who feel rejected and are so devastated that they retreat into seclusion from any social contact with others.

The following is an example:

Therapist: Jane, so what actually happened when you saw Doug last Saturday?

Jane: He dumped me. He said he started seeing someone else. What a fool I am. I have no judgment in men. They all turn out to be liars or they leave me. Maybe there is nothing wrong with them. Maybe it's me. If I were enough, why would they leave? Why would they be looking for someone else?

Therapist: Jane, I don't know what his reasons were for leaving, but I care about you and want to help you through this.

Jane: I am so upset I feel sick. I wish he'd talked to me and given me and the relationship a chance. He probably didn't think I was worth it.

Therapist: You are a good person and I'm sorry you didn't get more of a chance to work things out with Doug.

Jane: You are paid to like me or at least fake it. I keep getting dumped, so maybe even you can't fix what is wrong with me.

Jane is sinking into depression and loss of self-esteem. *The pain of being left obscures her capacity for being rational.* She is desperately trying to find a way to understand why this has happened to her, even if it means blaming herself.

This is what Jane needs to hear and believe: "We are all flawed. There is no perfect way to be or look that will guarantee that you won't get left. It is important to accept your imperfections, to validate yourself just as you are. This is vital to maintaining self-esteem, because out there lurking in the single world is a guy or gal with a bad haircut or rotten personality who, given the chance, may reject you. If this happens to you, you must be able to say to yourself, "I hate getting dumped, it hurts and it's embarrassing, but it doesn't say that I am so flawed that I caused the rejection or that I will continue to be rejected forever."

It means, "Someone didn't like me or want to stay with me or was too chicken to tough it out and really work on a relationship." The rejection usually has more to do with them and their expectations for a relationship than it has to do with you. Who wants to stay in a relationship with a person who is either too critical, wants to change you or is unable to maintain consistent fulfillment and acceptance of you?

When you get rejected, it may help to visualize the rejecter one year later desperately lonely, eating a frozen pizza alone while watching old reruns of "Bonanza." Or maybe imagine him/her desperately trying to find your phone number, regretting the day they broke off with you. You can see him/her calling you and hearing your outgoing message:

"I'll be out of town indefinitely visiting the Greek Islands with the Love Of My Life. We will undoubtedly experience other far-off lands before we return. We will let our passions lead the way. As a result, I will not be reachable. Leave a message, but I have no idea when I will get it...."

You'll find this slightly revengeful thinking can perk you up enough so you can give dating another try.

WHY DO WE RESIST COMMITMENT?

For many people, the issue of commitment ruins a relationship. Why is this? Because commitment is a wake-up call to grow up. Commitment involves compromising, negotiating and being unselfish more often than many single people are used to. It can feel like a threat to individuality and freedom. It can seem as inviting as electrolysis or a tooth extraction.

Because of these fears and issues, resistance to commitment seems self-preserving and reasonable. What people need to understand is that commitment is hard, but like a strenuous workout that we are tempted to avoid, it yields benefits that are not gained from any other situation. Some of these benefits are:

1. intimacy

2. safe, satisfying sex

3. companionship

4. support for your goals and dreams

5. an opportunity to give and enhance self-respect

If any one of these sound good to you, and are lacking in your life, keep reading—with a positive attitude.

COMMITMENT PHOBIC EXAMPLE #1

Dave is dating Mary whom he says he adores. He has been dating her for one year. On one of their Saturday night dates, Mary tells Dave that she would like to have more of a commitment. She wants them to be exclusive, discuss future mutual goals and be more accountable to each other regarding schedules, financial matters and other personal business.

Within one week of this conversation, Dave starts finding fault with Mary. He withdraws physically and starts complaining to friends about her. When she confronts him on the change of attitude, he denies that there is a problem. He continues to be distant and is unwilling to discuss commitment issues. Eventually, he stops calling her. He starts dating someone new.

COMMITMENT PHOBIC EXAMPLE #2

Nancy has been seeing Bill for nine months. She sees him often, is sexual with him but has a lot of complaints about him. When confronted by her friends as to why she stays with him, she says that he is fun and nice.

Bill really likes her and says he wants to make a commitment. She changes the subject when he brings it up. When he confronts her, she tells him she needs more time. She doesn't reveal her complaints to him, so there is no chance to resolve issues. The relationship fades into a casual thing and ends with no clarity. She starts dating someone new.

Dave and Nancy have a problem. They are afraid to get deeply involved with anyone. They are comfortable dating, but uncomfortable with some of the most basic aspects of commitment, such as:

1. being sexually faithful
2. being accountable to someone regarding time, money
3. sacrificing for someone else
4. becoming as interested in their partners as they are in themselves

RESISTING COMMITMENT WITH NEW PARTNERS

Most of the time when people resist committing to new relationships (ones that do not have a history of negative experiences), it means they have been hurt and traumatized in the past by relationships that promised love and closeness, but did not deliver. This resistance may sometimes seem illogical. Example: John's wife left him after five years of marriage. She started a relationship with a friend of his. He had no idea that she was not happy or that she was capable of being so deceitful.

The shock didn't wear off, but after a year-and-a-half, John decided to start dating again. John met Alice and liked her very much. They had been dating for six months exclusively. A typical conversation between them often sounded like this:

Alice: I tried to call you last night because I wanted to tell you about my raise. I was so excited. You weren't home. Where did you go?

John: I was out. It is no big deal.

Alice: I am not saying it was a big deal, I was worried. You are always home by 10:00 p.m.

John: I wasn't aware I had a curfew. I won't be put on a leash.

At this point in the conversation, Alice would not only like to smack John with a leash, but was tempted to feed him dog kibble at their next home-cooked meal. Alice wondered, "What is wrong with him? Couldn't he hear that I was worried about him? Couldn't he hear that I wanted to share something exciting that had happened to me? Why would he think I was trying to control him?"

Alice is unaware of John's history and confused about his reactions, which are explained by his trauma. For John, the idea of close accountability made him feel married. He felt shamed by what had happened to him in his marriage. He had negative knee-jerk reactions to any requests to give in areas that made him feel married. John needs to overcome the trauma in his past relationship. He is emotionally injured and incapable of seeing a woman for whom she is; he fears that any new partner will repeat the actions of his ex-wife.

RESISTING COMMITMENT TO OLD PARTNERS (GIVING IT ANOTHER TRY)

At times, resistance may be a blessing in disguise. It's a way to protect yourself from getting hurt *again* by the same person—you know, the same person who gave you half-dead flowers for your birthday, two days *after* your birthday? This would also be the same one who begged you for a diamond watch to show your undying love and then left you a month after the gift (and, of course, did not offer to return it). These people's photographs should be on dart boards, and you should be thankful you're not bound to them anymore.

If the history with your old partner was painful and destructive, find someone new. Yes, people do change and a reconciliation may be possible, but if you are resisting committing to it again, you may not be up for the hard work ahead of you. It is O.K. to resist that kind of a choice and instead chose an easier path. You don't have to try to trust someone again who put your heart in a blender and pushed the "frappe" button.

FEAR OF LOSS OF SELF & PERSONAL FREEDOM

Believe it or not, we have worked with many clients who worry more about the loss of freedom to eat dinner at home in their birthday suits than they do about the possibility of being permanently alone without a partner or a family. We don't know how the freedom to eat naked alone in front of your TV became more of a priority than having your higher emotional and physical needs meant —needs that only a committed relationship can offer. Think about this for a moment: Maybe the loss of certain things about you or ways that you have been living would be an improvement!

The reality is that in a mature, committed relationship we *are* required to alter our behavior or our thinking at times. In order for the dynamic between ourselves and our partners to be stable and compatible, both people must learn to be open and flexible. This flexibility does not mean that you completely abandon your values or opinions. It does not mean that you change your basic personality or your goals.

FINDING THE BALANCE BETWEEN PERSONAL FREEDOM & COMMITMENT

◊ You become open to not getting your way all of the time, without getting angry.

◊ You learn to enjoy pleasing your partner as much as you enjoy taking care of yourself.

◊ You learn how to accept change that is not always initiated by you.

◊　You respect your partner's personality as much as your own.

◊　You remain aware that there are mutual issues that require mutual input and agreement.

◊　You learn how to stay true to yourself at times, without discounting your partner.

EXAMPLE: LOSS OF SELF

Glen continually worried that if he made a commitment, he would never be able to be spontaneously selfish again, that he would never play golf again or choose to spend time alone over being with his partner.

A typical conversation with Glen sounded like this:

Glen:　　Sure, I would like to get married and have kids. But a wife and kids would always have to come first. It seems like I would lose a lot that I now treasure about my life.

Therapist: That is a myth about marriage and committed relationships in general. A healthy relationship considers the feelings and needs of *both* partners.

Glen:　　I don't believe that. That is not the way it was with my parents.

Glen is not ready for commitment. He believes he will lose his autonomy. In his mind, he is making a logical decision to stay out of committed relationships in order to avoid experiencing a loss of self.

EXAMPLE DIALOGUE: LOSS OF FREEDOM OF CHOICE

Sarah fears that she will not be able to appropriately negotiate, compromise, or hold her ground in a committed relationship.

Sarah:　I don't want to buy a house now. We just got married.

Bill:　　It would really benefit me—and us—if I bought property and became eligible for the tax deduction.

Sarah:　I would rather save our money or travel together before we become saddled with the responsibility of a house. I would refuse to sign the papers.

Bill:　　I know it's a scary prospect, but we have to buy something or we will have more financial problems in the long run.

Sarah: O.K. I guess you're saying that I have no choice but to comply or I will cause our financial ruin. (Anger and resentment are setting in. She is already thinking of ignoring him for the rest of the evening.)

Sarah is not ready for commitment. She does not stand up for herself. She gives in. Instead, she could have:

1. tried to negotiate with Bill on other available options.

2. asked him questions that would have helped her understand and maybe better accept the decision to buy a home.

3. said "No" rather than allowing herself to feel trapped and resentful.

At this point, she may be considering whether a committed relationship is something she really wants. To show you the extent of her desperation, she began longing for the days when guys would dump her for ordering an expensive dinner item on the menu. She found that she felt a sense of relief in realizing that being rejected meant she would not lose any of the control she had over her life.

HOW PERSONAL PROBLEMS LIMIT YOUR READINESS FOR COMMITMENT

If you're a mess, your relationships will be a mess. If you have thoughts such as, "I don't make enough money for anyone to want me for a spouse" or " I am not good-looking enough and I am sure I will get left someday," you are smart to stay out of a committed relationship. It will end up in disaster because you will sabotage it due to your insecurities.

You should resist commitment when you have any of the following:

◊   emotional problems

◊   substance abuse problems

◊   existing commitment to someone else

◊   negative attitudes about commitment

It is difficult to focus on someone else's feelings and long-term goals when your thinking is unclear. It is wise to resist commitment until these problems can be resolved or brought under control.

You resist commitment because you know you are not ready. When you realize that you are holding back because you will not be able to meet the normal standards of a relationship, you are acting in a healthy way. Keeping relationships at the casual level will be better in the long run for you and your partner. But before you pull out the stop sign, know you don't have to be perfect to be in a relationship. We are all flawed in some way.

It is important for people to be able to talk about their imperfections with candor and acceptance. Many clients resist making a commitment out of fear that they will be "found out" once they become more intimate. That fear and resistance sounds like this:

Joan: I can't imagine being married and being expected to always shower and bathe with a spouse. I like the dating limits—where I can go home or send him home or make up rules that as a wife would be considered weird, but as a date would be acceptable. I like the relationship on that level.

Therapist: But what about the benefits of marriage and experiencing more commitment, more blending of your life with his? Does any of that appeal to you?

Joan: Yeah, but all that other stuff goes with it and I would be so uncomfortable with it. And what if he expects to use the bathroom to wash his face when I am going to the bathroom. I would hate that. No thank you.

Therapist: You sound very shy and private about certain physical intimacies. None of these boundaries render you weird or crazy. They should, however, be explored and understood. You may be able to eliminate them—or maybe not. Learning why you have certain boundaries or limits can help you decide to change them.

Joan resists commitment because of fear that in some way it will be uncomfortable and humiliating. These were strong feelings for her. Because of them, she continued to push men away.

Most healthy people respect their partner's boundaries, eccentricities and sensibilities. They are aware that they have their own "quirks," as all people do. People who criticize or shame us are mean, critical and immature. If they were healthy people, they would just end the relationship without blaming or shaming, and do it with acceptance and respect for you. If you are healthy, you have low tolerance for any lesser treatment.

REDUCING THE FEAR OF COMMITMENT

It takes work to become less fearful and more open and positive about commitment. Such work is not mysterious or impossible, although it may be uncomfortable at times. Yet, if you want a committed relationship, you'll find you can do it.

To become less resistant to commitment you must:

◊ work on becoming more assertive

◊ learn more about the realities and benefits of commitment and marriage

◊ make a pact with yourself not to abandon yourself in the name of love and commitment

◊ develop tolerance for the pressure of someone else's needs and expectations

When we become more assertive, we can say "No" and keep to our personal boundaries. When we learn that a good relationship is about acceptance and respect for each other, we can begin to trust that we will not be injured by our partner. You learn to say, "This is a non-negotiable part of me." If you can do this, you do not have to resist commitment but, rather, you can enter into it with personal strength. Remember that if you want to eat peanut butter and mayonnaise sandwiches as appetizers before a Chinese meal, do it. Your partner will have to learn to look the other way or take a bite and try out your tastes!

BASIC TO A RELATIONSHIP IS THE ABILITY TO:

1. stick with problems and have the patience to see issues through to a positive result.

2. be resilient and not let a fight or disagreement discourage you.

3. be open to admitting that you are wrong (trust us, you will not die from it).

4. have realistic expectations of yourself, your partner and your relationships.

These expectations require that you be emotionally mature and willing to work on behalf of your relationship. If you still believe that commitment should be easy or one-sided (in your favor), you won't be successful at committed relationships.

SUMMARY

Both sexes resist commitment. They equally fear being rejected or feeling unsuccessful at relationships. The willingness to identify, address and find solutions to your fears opens up the possibility of intimacy and commitment.

Old hurt and trauma can build walls that keep people as far away from you as the moon. Face the past and learn how not to let it color your view of new partners or yourself. Talk to others who have been successful and happy in making commitments. Learn from them how to do it—and then do it.

Discover new ways to assert yourself with people. The less you fear they will control you, the less you will feel you have to avoid getting close. Being assertive does not mean creating constant conflict. It means setting forth the ground rules for yourself and asking and expecting to have them considered and accepted. *You will never find the fulfillment you long for if you resist commitment.* Instead of seeing commitment as a trap that was specifically built to ruin your chances for happiness, see it as an opportunity to experience love, nurturing and intimacy. Staying alone and losing out on companionship and romance is a choice that we hope you will no longer continue to make.

HEALTHY DATING RULE #6

Overcome your fears of rejection and vulnerability by figuring out why you are afraid and taking steps to meet new, healthy, single people.

CHAPTER SEVEN

Foolish Dating Mistake # 7

YOU INTERVIEW FOR A SPOUSE

QUIZ:

Before your first date you demand that they Fed Ex:

1. their credit and medical reports.
2. their family tree dating back to the 14th century.
3. a letter of reference from every one of their former partners.

Interviewing-for-a-spouse is what is happening when you ask probing questions of your new date in a way that sounds as if he or she is being considered for a job. Some people are subtle about making inquiries, while others are downright obvious. Many people do not realize they are acting like obnoxious reporters. Usually, the reason we interview is to learn quickly whether the applicant is right for the job. Reflect on the possibility that you conduct interviews of your dates to see if they're right for the position of permanent partner in your life.

BASIC INTERVIEW FOR A SPOUSE
TECHNIQUE " 101"

Lisa (Interviewer): So how long have you been in California?

Terry: Ten years.

Lisa: Do you like it? Are you planning to remain here?
        (Inner Interviewer Thought: If he's planning to leave, I want
        to know.)

Terry: Oh, I love it. I live in a great house with a view and I plan to
        stick around.

Lisa: You own your own house?
        (Inner Interviewer Thought: Does he have property and/or
        financial resources?)

Terry: No, I rent it.

Lisa: So, tell me about what you do for a living?

Terry: I'm a stockbroker. I find it exciting and kind of different
        each day.

Lisa: How long have you been doing it?
        (Inner Interviewer Thought: Is he stable and trustworthy?)

Terry: Actually, only about five years now. Before that I owned a
        construction company, but I sold it. I wanted to try something
        different.

Lisa: (The Interviewer is busy trying to decide what that really
        means in terms of her future with him.)

What is next in this conversation? Is Lisa going to now ask if he
loves his mother and what the relationship with his father is? She
could certainly try and establish his mental health as long as she is
on an interviewing roll! Lisa is the obnoxious version of this dating
mistake, but the mistake itself is not uncommon.

People tell us all the time that they want to get a few questions
out of the way quickly before they waste any more time on that
person. We can understand the reasoning, but it is a big mistake.
The information that you gather on a first or second date is
important, but it is out of context relative to the whole person you
are getting to know.

The most common example of this is when dates ask if you have
ever been married before. There is no right answer to this question.
If you have been married before, they want to know why it didn't
work out. The extensive details about why a marriage died are
difficult to explain to someone you barely know. Frequently, you
come off sounding either flip about it or destroyed over it. If you
have never been married, people fantasize the worst reasons why
not—from fear of commitment to gender confusion! Once again, to

put the explanation in context, you would have to get too personal and revealing.

Having a few cups of coffee or lunches with someone before deciding whether or not to put more time into getting to know them is *not* a waste. It is a great investment. If you choose to interview instead, you may put off the exact kind of person for whom you are searching, or you may end up judging that person prematurely. Become aware of the ways in which you might be doing this. Begin to have more relaxed and natural conversations. The information you think you need will reveal itself without the need to bring out a pen and pad and go down the checklist.

THE COMPULSION TO QUESTION

Asking a few general questions about your date is polite and shows your interest and ability to pay attention to others. This is a healthy way to begin and to continue conversation while getting to know someone.

EXAMPLE OF GOOD QUESTIONING

John: Are you from New York originally?

Lori: Well, no. I was born in Ohio and came here for a couple of reasons. I thought New York would be better for my career as a writer and I also love to travel—and it's easier from here.

John: I love to travel, too. Where have you been so far?

Lori feels flattered by John's interest in her life, yet John does not asked any super personal or pointed questions containing a hidden agenda. He is merely chatting and getting to know Lori—slowly but surely.

EXAMPLE #2 OF GOOD QUESTIONING

Judy met Tom when as a police officer he took her statement after she was a witness to a minor car accident. He called her a few days later and they agreed to get together for some coffee.

Judy: I've never had the opportunity to talk with a cop before. I'm interested in hearing about your job. Did you always want to work in law enforcement?

Tom: Yeah, I did. I would always watch the cop shows and think the characters must have a great life. I thought only of the excitement then. Of course, now I know about the stress, the long hours and the bad press! Seriously, I do love my job and it is always different every minute, but it's a lot harder than I thought.

POOR CHOICE QUESTION WITH HIDDEN AGENDA

Judy: Do you find it difficult to work hard and handle stress?

GOOD CHOICE QUESTION— WITHOUT THE HIDDEN AGENDA

Judy: I've heard that it's a stressful job—what's a typical day like?
Tom: (shares some day-to-day details)
        No. I want to continue in my career.
        (with a grin) I like it overall, but I also like to complain from time to time.
Judy: Oh, me too. What is your biggest pet peeve?

Now they go on to compare funny but annoying aspects of their jobs and get to know each other again, from a more indirect approach. They are learning about each other through general conversation.

GUIDELINES FOR TURNING INTERROGATION INTO CONVERSATION

Try not to ask too many personal questions in a row:
1. Are your parents alive?
2. Do you have a good relationship with them?
3. Were you married before?
4. Why didn't it work out?
5. Where is he or she now and are you still friends?
6. Do you make a good living?
7. Would you like to have children?
8. How many children would you like to have?
9. Do I sound like a detective agency?

Accept that you cannot always learn in the course of the first or second date whether or not you want to date this person long-term.

Attempting to invasively gather information about a person is very stressful—so relax and only ask the more general questions; e.g., "Where have you traveled?" This will give you a lot of information, but in a more subtle and enjoyable way. Examples of other general questions are:

1. Do you enjoy your work?
2. What do you enjoy doing on your time off?
3. What's your opinion on [something you have just done or seen of interest].

WHY DO YOU INTERVIEW?

The compulsion to interview is strong because it gives you quick information. Information gathered this way, however, lacks soul. Why do some go after it?

YOU ARE INSECURE

Perhaps you are a person who is basically insecure. Individuals who are insecure need to check everything out for safety features as soon as possible. Is their date safe to get involved with? Many people feel bad about some part of their life and need to see how the other person feels about it before they get rejected.

Gary was in a tight bind financially after some poor investments and he realized it would be a long-term struggle to get out of the situation. When he went on dates, he manipulated the conversation around finding out how important money was to his date. This financial insecurity of Gary's was very difficult for dates to deal with. In an attempt to protect himself from "women who wouldn't want him anyway," Gary annoyed many good prospects by playing this kind of game. If he'd just been himself and allowed the date to evolve, he'd have risked less and possibly learned more about his date.

People do not enjoy being interviewed. And even if they are not aware that a fact-finding mission is going on, they may be responding in ways that are left to your own interpretation since your true agenda is hidden!

YOU ARE A CONTROL FREAK

If knowledge is power, it makes sense that control freaks would want to gain as much knowledge about their date as quickly as they can. Some people get their self-esteem from being "in charge." They have to know and control everything, including information. These people feel safest when they know all and you know little about them. You are on a "need to know basis" with them. Control freaks may view your sharing as an indication of vulnerability; on the other hand, they like to keep their own defenses up and their information in. Control freaks think along the lines of, "Let me find out if this person is worthy of my time." Then they control and manipulate the conversation accordingly. It is almost impossible for control demons to just let loose and enjoy events as they happen. The truth is they lack the inner strength to get up if they fall, so they make sure they never fall.

YOU ARE NOT ABLE TO ENJOY THE JOURNEY

Another reason people mistakenly interview on dates is that they lack the ability to see the importance of the journey and, instead, focus only on the goal. A good relationship or marriage is a great goal, but getting there has a lot to do with learning what you need to know to be a healthy partner. Each false start gives you something, even if it feels like the biggest waste of time. It is possible that people pass through our lives giving us experiences and knowledge that will be necessary later. Some stay a long time and others pass through in a date or two. All of them play a part in our growth and our ability to handle situations.

If we could view dating as the first phase of a journey that is necessary to prepare us for the next phase—a committed relationship—we would be more open to the value of it instead of viewing bad dates as a waste of our time.

Being open to the idea of the "journey" adds to your availability for the serendipitous aspects of life to happen and not go unnoticed. You have to commit to the whole journey and not get stuck at the bus stops along the way. Everyone you meet is not a potential spouse. Thinking of dates as a lot of wasted time misses the point. Everyone you meet is a potential bus ride to your future mate, so try to get something out of the dating trip.

YOU HAVE NO MORE PATIENCE

This brings us to the next issue that drives people to the interview-your-date-within-an-inch-of-his-or-her-life technique. If you lack patience, you will have a difficult time moving through the journey and enjoying and learning from the little, but not insignificant, things. Having patience is a huge problem because dating tests you in many ways:

1. All kinds of people are out there and many can annoy you right out of whatever patience you have left.

2. Some individuals are just bad dates and their lack of consideration can easily make you want to drive right off the dating road.

3. We often feel some kind of time pressure, whether from ourselves, our peers or family—or that much-discussed "clock" that you hear ticking.

INCREASE YOUR PATIENCE BY KNOWING WHO YOU ARE LOOKING FOR

One way to stretch your patience is to get an idea of what you are looking for in a mate. Patients always laugh in our faces when we suggest that they write a Future Mate Wish List. This list includes all of the major characteristics, both mental and physical, that you need in a spouse. "Need" is the important word here. It helps to be able to distinguish what we really "need" in a partner in order to be happy versus what we might "want" as an added bonus to the deal.

Jeff felt he "needed" to marry a woman of his faith. He believed he could not be happy otherwise. One day, after years of being single and actively seeking his mate, he married out of his faith. His wife was willing to agree to help him raise their children in his faith since she was not really affiliated with another religion. He felt disappointed at times that his wife did not fully understand his holidays or some of his cultural ways, but despite it, he was happy.

He had wanted the religions to be the same, but ultimately a compromise was reached and he did not "need" it to be exactly as he had dreamed to be happy.

HOW CAN YOU TELL THE DIFFERENCE BETWEEN A NEED & A WANT?

A need is something we must have to feel satisfied and fulfilled with a person or a situation. Every person has a set of needs that is specific to them. For example, some people need to have their partners share the same interests. Without this, they are unhappy in their relationships. For others, having similar interests would be icing on the cake, yet are not necessary. A want is something we can live without, but having it would improve the quality of our life.

HOW TO MAKE YOUR "FUTURE MATE WISH LIST"

First, try listing everything you could ever possibly want. Make sure to include physical, personality and character traits. Also, add in interests, work or hobbies. Here's an example given by Tamra:

☺Rich

☺Handsome

! Tall

☺Great Hair

! Athletic

! Romantic

☆Enjoys Sex

☆Open Minded

☆Politically Moderate

! Christian

! Solvent

☺Runs Own Business Or Is An Executive

☺Speaks A Foreign Language

! American

! Loves To Travel

☺Likes To Do Some Daily Things Together (cook, laundry, etc.)

☆ Strong Character (honest and trustworthy)

☆ Sensitive (good listener)

☆ Willing To Talk About How He Feels

☺Spends Time With His Own Friends

☺Likes Baseball

! Likes To Eat Out

☆ Doesn't Drink Or Use Drugs

! Doesn't Smoke

☆ Funny And Laughs Easily

! Spontaneous

After your list is made, please go back over it the next day and then make a symbol/notation next to each item (after careful thought) rating the items:

☆ URGENT—I absolutely need this in order to be happy and satisfied. This item is non-negotiable.

! IMPORTANT—I would like to have this trait; it would enhance our relationship, but it is not a deal breaker.

☺ICING ON THE CAKE—This would be fun, but I don't have to have it at all, it's just a good wish.

As Tamra went over her list, she was then able to see what she truly *needs* (urgent) what she *wants* (important) and what is purely icing on the cake.

It is important to realize that all of your wishes cannot come true. But most of them can and, once you have a clear picture of what you need, you are more likely to find it. Being open and flexible about it is important, but if you really want your patience to endure, you will refrain from dating people who are clearly wrong for you from the start. These "wrong-way" relationships take a lot out of us and diminish the patience necessary for the long journey.

Sarah, a Jewish woman with quite a religious commitment, came into therapy because of her relationship with Roy, a non-Jewish man. Each was hoping that the other would convert to the other's religion one day. There were other problems having to do with views on family, use of money and more. Further exploration revealed that the real reason Sarah felt she needed to be with Roy had to do with lack of patience. Sarah wanted to get married and was on her last breath when it came to dating—she had run out of patience.

It is not as unusual as you might think to run out of steam and settle for much less than what you want. You can't have it all but you don't need to settle for hardly anything, either. Patience for the longer journey will allow you to pick dates more carefully, have a more accurate idea of what you are looking for and keep in mind that it is the journey that is important and not just the destination.

Although you may be worn down by the dating scene, which is understandable, you also could be the type of person who is just impatient in every area of your life. Consider the following statements and answer True or False:

1. I hate traffic lights when they turn red.
2. Microwaves do not work fast enough.
3. Everyone should answer their phone by the second ring.
4. Everyone drives too slowly all the time.

5. Elevators are for people with nothing but time on their hands.

6. I can't click my remote control fast enough.

7. Standing in line for anything makes me feel like part of a herd of cattle.

8. I want my hair to grow out by tomorrow and to lose fifteen pounds by Friday.

9. I wish there were drive-through Laundromats.

10. When learning anything new, I have to be able to get it in ten minutes or less, or I wasn't meant to know it.

If you answered "True" to any of these statements, it is time to take a look at your usual level of patience. To be successful at dating, you will have to boost the "P" level in your life. Listed are some of the ways to raise that level in your daily life:

1. Give people a break wherever you go.
   They may be having their worst day and are usually not that stupid.

2. Get some sleep.
   When you are tired all the time you tend to be more irritable.

3. Get some relaxation.
   Take some deep breaths during the day. Read a great magazine, rent an old movie, take a short nap, go out and enjoy nature, take a walk.

4. Get some exercise.
   Release stress with something you enjoy doing.

5. Have some fun.
   If you can't remember the last time you had a fun day, it's time to get reacquainted with the lighter side of yourself. Having fun lightens the spirit—so schedule it in.

6. Get some spiritual underpinning to your life.
   The foundation of most religious and spiritual disciplines is the recognition that patience and understanding are essential ways to help you cope.

7. Fight perfectionism.
   It is a nasty habit and robs you of patience for yourself and for others.

SUMMARY

Dating can test anyone's patience. But interviewing your dates for the possibility of permanent status in your life can be a Foolish Dating Mistake. It can kill any chance you may have had with that someone, who might actually have been right for you.

If you find yourself thinking, "I'd better ask a few important questions and see what my date answers before I get too interested," tell yourself to relax and enjoy the activity that you are sharing. The information you need *is* important, but if your way of gathering it is more reminiscent of weeding out applicants for a job than enjoying someone new on a social level, you may be the one who is eliminated before the benefits can begin to accrue.

HEALTHY RULE #7

Try to let information unfold on a date. Stick with more general questions, and develop patience for the process.

CHAPTER EIGHT

Foolish Dating Mistake #8

·⁓☾☉

YOU ARE CONSISTENTLY UNASSERTIVE

QUIZ:

You're too passive if you:

1. never order your own food in a restaurant.
2. refuse to tell your date to stop standing on your foot.
3. would rather scrub your bathtub with a toothbrush than say "no" to anyone or anything at any time.

Good communication is the basis for healthy relationships. Poor communication is the iceberg that sinks the ship. Unassertiveness is a form of poor communication because it renders the relationship false, boring, stuck, and dissatisfying. Unassertiveness leads you into distasteful situations, such as:

1. being kissed by someone you would rather be playing scrabble with
2. being touched by someone you are not attracted to and that you are possibly even scared of
3. listening to someone talk about something that bores or offends you

4. avoiding constructive confrontations that could enhance your relationship

UNASSERTIVENESS LIMITS RELATIONSHIP FULFILLMENT

Unassertive people are unhappy and frustrated in their relationships. They do not get their needs met and they feel angry at not being heard (even though they are not saying anything). In a healthy relationship, each one has to carry his or her own weight in the area of communication. The results of not speaking up for yourself can cause situations that are worse than staying home alone on those long "I-will-never-date-again" sabbaticals.

Rebecca took one of those sabbaticals after an interlude with Evan, a man she dated many years ago:

"Evan started to lean forward, coming closer to me. He closed his eyes and a weird moan came out of his mouth. A moan that said, 'I have been waiting for you my whole life, Rebecca.'

"'Oh no!' I thought, 'Here comes the kiss. The kiss that I do not want—that I dread.'

"It was our fifth date, so an innocent kiss was not out of line for Evan to pursue. I closed my eyes and also moaned, but for a different reason—mine was a substitute for speaking up for myself. It was a moan that said, 'I don't want to, but I can't stop it from happening.' It was a moan of weakness, of unassertiveness.

"Before I knew it, I felt my cheek being sucked so hard that I feared my lips and right ear would soon be awkwardly touching each other. Worse than this sensation (and believe me, I was not having fun), was the realization that my lips were the next target for assault. Then it happened and I slipped into some kind of haze, some kind of unassertive vacuum. I felt sorry for myself and angry at myself all at the same time. This experience was a test of my ability to be assertive and I failed miserably."

The kiss was finally over and an awkward silence befell Evan and Rebecca until she finally spoke:

Rebecca: Well, it's getting late and I have to get up early. Thanks for everything.

Evan: O.K., Rebecca. I'll call you tomorrow and see you soon.
Rebecca: Good Night.

Rebecca had so much to say but did not know how to express herself. What froze her up the most was the fact that Evan was such a nice guy. She didn't know how to say, "I have to stop seeing you" or "I am not feeling close in that way." She didn't know when to do it or how to time it; both her physical behavior and verbal ability had literally become frozen. She was being controlled by her desire not to hurt Evan. She was trying to give it more time, but the truth was there were no romantic feelings there.

Remember that in Chapter Three we said that not all situations will develop chemistry? When, after reasonable attempts, there is no sign of chemistry, it is appropriate to end a relationship rather than to unassertively keep suffering through "a kiss from hell" in the name of being a nice person.

In the situation with Evan, it is apparent that Rebecca should have taken better care of her feelings during the development of the relationship. She let things escalate until she found herself kissing someone whom she felt absolutely no romantic feelings for. She was young and uninformed regarding assertiveness skills.

She learned from that experience. Next time she found herself being pursued by a pair of lips that made the hair on her neck stand up (not out of passion, mind you) she asserted herself, yet still was able to be kind and gentle in her rejection of this gesture:

Rebecca : (placing her hands gently on Jim's shoulder and taking a short step backward)
          Jim, I'm not comfortable enough to get physical at this point.

Jim: What is wrong? Have I done something?

Rebecca: No, you haven't done anything wrong. I'm just not feeling the way I know I need to feel in order to get physical with you in a romantic way.

Jim: How long will it take you?

Rebecca: I don't know when or if it will change. I would like to spend more time dating and see what develops.

Jim: I guess we can try and see how things go.

This conversation is honest, clear and leaves room for whatever the outcome will be. It may be uncomfortable to tell someone that you have limited feelings for him or her, and that you want to take things slowly, but it is fair, mature and honest. You notice that Jim did not lose control, or take it personally, but asked questions, accepted what was and decided to hang in there to see if more feelings would develop.

DO NOT GO OVERBOARD WITH ASSERTIVENESS

We are not saying that being 100 percent assertive about what you are thinking and feeling all the time is appropriate. If your date shows up wearing a red shirt and you hate red, it would be unnecessary and obnoxious to say, "I have to tell you I really hate red; I just thought I would tell you." Who cares and what's the point? Assertiveness is most important when the assertion would enhance or advance the intimacy in the relationship. It can be a turn-off to constantly listen to what your partner's opinion is on everything. Use judgment and speak up when it really matters. Honesty and assertiveness without compassion are really only cruelty.

ASSERTIVENESS DEFINED

The dictionary defines assertiveness as the expression of thoughts, feelings, opinions and ideas, both verbally and nonverbally. Unassertiveness is the opposite behavior. It means keeping things bottled up inside you. It means making another person more important than yourself by letting their thoughts and feelings dominate the relationship.

Evan had all the power. He was being assertive, expressing his feelings in a physical way. It wasn't his job to read Rebecca's mind and take care of her feelings. Without speaking up, she left room for him to assume that what he wanted to be true was true.

THE BASICS OF ASSERTIVE BEHAVIOR

◊ Use the word "I" when describing how you feel. (Speaking in general terms about how "other people feel" or "they" feel does not commit you to how *you* honestly feel.)

◊ State the facts about what you are referring to. (When Rebecca told Jim how she felt, she referred to "getting physical in a romantic way" so he knew specifically not to pursue that behavior with her.)

◊ Make requests of the person if appropriate or necessary. ("Jim, please stop trying to kiss me. I need to talk to you.")

◊ Ask questions if appropriate or necessary. ("Jim, what are your expectations for this relationship?")

◊ Be able to say "No." (Merely hinting at "No" leaves room for misunderstanding.)

◊ Be willing to leave the situation if you do not feel heard or respected. (Do not worry about being rude. If you let a person know that you are leaving because you feel uncomfortable or unsafe, you are being considerate of both you and them.)

NIGHTMARE DATING SCENARIOS THAT WE ALL DREAD

EXPERIENCING THE UNWELCOME TOUCH

Ben felt himself tense up every time Lynn caressed the hair from his forehead. He liked Lynn and was even attracted to her, but this particular gesture of hers really bothered him. He didn't like the way it felt. It seemed that when she was doing it she wasn't listening to what he was saying at the time. He wanted to tell her, but he didn't know how. He knew two things very clearly: He wanted her to stop touching his hair and he did not want to hurt her or push her away from him because he was interested and attracted to her. He opted to remain unassertive. Time passed and she continued to do it and he became increasingly withdrawn from her. He started sitting further away from her and was self-conscious about it. She finally noticed something was wrong as *she* confronted *him:*

Lynn: Ben, why are you sitting so far away and being so quiet?

Ben: Everything's fine. I didn't even notice I was doing that.

Lynn: Well, Ben, it is obvious to me. You are so far away, I can't even touch you when we're speaking to each other.

Ben: I'm sorry, I will stop doing those things now that you have made me aware.

This unassertive behavior on Ben's part is leading this relationship into the dumpster. How long do you think Ben is going to want to cringe and be irritated on his dates with Lynn? How long will it take for him to convince himself that he does not like Lynn at all, as a way of avoiding the assertive confrontation? We would say that after the above conversation occurred, he is getting ready to disappear from her life, probably leaving her to wonder what went wrong. If he didn't confront her on the hair touching, his unassertive persona certainly is not going to sit down and break up with her in a clear, honest way. Lynn is about to experience the "Houdini Act," also known as "I can't believe he just stopped calling."

Here is what it would sound like if Ben had pushed through his discomfort with assertiveness and talked to Lynn instead of verbally "bailing."

Ben: (Lynn brushes Ben's hair from his forehead for what feels to him like the thousandth time,)
       Lynn, I have to tell you something. I really do not like it when my hair is touched like that. I don't know why, but it does bother me and I have been afraid to say anything. I don't want to hurt you or get you mad.

Lynn: I'm sorry, Ben. You should have told me before; I would have stopped. But I will stop now. It was just a sign of affection, it's something I've always done with people. Sorry about that.

Ben: Actually, I think most people are O.K. with it. It's a thing with me about having my hair touched in that way while I'm talking with someone. Thanks for understanding.

Lynn: Sure Ben. It's no big deal and I'm glad you told me.

In words like this, you can take care of behaviors that are going on in your relationship that you do not like. When a guy's hand starts wandering up your leg and you are uncomfortable, you can either say, "Please stop" or "I am not comfortable with that" or use a nonverbal assertive technique and just remove his hand.

With assertiveness, you have to find a style and the words that are comfortable for you. We are providing you with examples of what to say. If they sound too "credentialed" for your taste, don't dismiss the whole concept. Find your own words and use them to speak out. You'll have more success if you feel comfortable with how you say what you have to say.

LISTENING TO THE BORING OR OFFENSIVE DATE

If you are an unassertive dater you have probably been in countless situations where you were so bored with the conversation that you considered faking a heart attack to escape the experience. Not all people are good conversationalists. And even if they are skilled in that area, they may not be talking about something that interests you. Most of us were raised to be "nice" and "polite." In our social behavior, this message usually meant to never interrupt someone when they were talking, to act interested even if you are totally bored and to lie by saying "yes" if someone asks you if it's all right with you if they continue on with what they're talking about. This early message about social behavior, coupled with a natural tendency to be shy or introverted, produces the "foolish" behavior that hinders the enjoyment of the dating experience.

Many people we have talked to say they would rather stay home alone than face the discomfort of confronting someone. The good news is that assertiveness does not have to destroy people's self-esteem or cause them to give up dating forever. If done in a positive way, assertiveness enhances intimacy. The deeper level of honesty allows for more closeness and more awareness of each other. Awareness of each other helps each person assess the compatibility that exists between them. A conversation that Lila had with Dan is a good example of how to face the boredom issue bravely and constructively:

Dan: (a stockbroker and overall nice guy with whom she is riding to the theater on their fourth date)
What a busy day I had. My phone rang off the hook. I was talking to Jane Sherwood about some stocks she wanted to buy. I was trying to explain to her why I thought she should buy and sell quickly on the textile stock she was interested in. She's a nice lady, but she talks too much about her kids. She has three boys....

Lila: (smiling and nodding, but thinking about which celebrities were on the "Tonight Show" later and what she would be eating for breakfast tomorrow)
Wow. She sounds like a difficult client in some ways. After all, you're always so busy and have limited time to...
(Dan interrupts)

Dan: I am so busy everyday. But this Mrs. Sherwood today, she kept asking why this and why that and then she asked about mutual funds. Now mutual funds are a totally different kind of investment...

Lila: (so bored her head feels like it is going to explode)
Oh, really? I am sure you helped her. You sound very good.

Lila was making every "nice" and "polite" unassertive mistake.

The key steps to being assertive are to:

1.   Honestly (and tactfully) express how you feel about what is being discussed.

Example: I am not very knowledgeable about or interested in investment at this point in my life—so I am getting a little lost in our conversation.

2.   Ask questions that may help you become more engaged in the conversation, if possible.

Example: How do you handle overly talkative clients?

(Maybe you can steal some of his techniques and use them on him.)

3.   Make attempts to redirect the conversation.

Example: Mrs. Sherwood does sound very difficult. Just think how thankful you should be that

your workday is over and we're on our way
to this great play. I can't wait to see it. Have
you read any of the reviews?

4. Try to become more interested in the conversation by
    asking questions that may challenge your intellect. (This
    assertive technique can eliminate boredom at times.)

    Example: Could you briefly summarize what mutual
                funds are?

5. Be blunt and direct if more subtle assertive attempts to
    change the subject fail. Admit feelings not only about the
    topic but about your reaction to the experience you are
    having.

    Example: I'm finding it hard to stay with this
                conversation. Between not being very
                interested in finance and being excited about
                seeing you and the play, I am not able to
                keep listening very well to what you are
                saying about Mrs. Sherwood.

This is undoubtedly very uncomfortable, and some of you
may be wondering what planet we really come from, but in some
situations with particularly persistent talkers, this will be your only
salvation.

The other conversationalist that challenges the unassertive
person to the core is the offender. Remember Barry from Chapter
Two? Here he is again, this time being rude and hurting Rebecca's
feelings quite regularly:

Barry: (upon entering her apartment)
         What color eye shadow is that? It's very red.

Rebecca: It's not red. Anyway, come and sit down. I will be ready
         in a minute.

Barry: (sitting down on the couch, then getting up and looking at
         the cushions and pressing them as if they are too lumpy)
         How old is this couch?

Rebecca: It's not that old. Try the chair.
         (At this point, she began to boil and, to her delight, she
         switched into an assertive mode)
         Barry, do you realize that the only words you have said
         since you arrived are critical ones? You haven't said hello
         or asked how I am doing. If you have that many

complaints about me or my house, maybe we shouldn't be going out.

Barry was not much of a communicator and he went into mental neutral with the above assertion. He then apologized. He was basically a good person, but he was critical and rude at times.

When Rebecca made a transition to living assertively in her relationships, the "Barrys" of the world were soon eliminated from her little black book.

AVOIDING CONFRONTATION

The dictionary defines confrontation this way:

to meet face to face, to encounter something to be dealt with, or an open conflict of opposing ideas.

Confrontation is not always negative or dramatic. If you think it is, or in your own life it has been, it is understandable why you avoid it. In reality, confrontation done correctly by two normal people (as normal as one can feel after being out there in the singles world for so long) moves a relationship to a deeper level.

WHY IS CONFRONTING SO IMPORTANT TO RELATIONSHIPS?

The goal of confrontation is to let someone know how you feel, what you want or what you do not want, or to ask a question to gain new knowledge and deeper understanding. If you cannot do this in your relationships, conflicts rarely get resolved and resentments can grow. For example, if you do not tell your partner that he or she has offended you in some way, you have to hold those feelings of being hurt or mad inside of you. This can only cause you stress and may cause you to withdraw from your partner.

We withdraw when we have bad feelings for a person and do not express and resolve the problem. In addition to this, if you do not confront someone on a behavior that you do not like, there is a good chance that he or she will keep doing it. Confrontation, if done correctly, brings about the resolution of differences or hurt feelings and creates a stronger bond between two people.

AVOIDANCE OF CONFRONTATION DIALOGUE

On your fifth date with Maria, she makes a joke that has racial overtones to it. You immediately feel uncomfortable and yet decide to say nothing to avoid what you fear will be an uncomfortable, negative confrontation. This kind of joke or reference from Maria happens again. You remain silent, but at this point, you are beginning to make assumptions about her. You think, "She is a racist. She is mean and uncaring about people."

The process of breaking up is underway. Maybe that is the right course to be considering. Maybe Maria is all of those things. But maybe she isn't. Maybe she is unaware of how offended you are. Maybe she is trying to reveal a sense of humor in order to attract you and she heard these jokes from someone else. Maybe she doesn't believe any of the negative inferences these jokes make. Maybe she is just using bad judgment. The truth cannot be known without a confrontation.

HEALTHY CONFRONTATION DIALOGUE

People often exit a relationship at the point of confrontation. This is how we believe many relationships that have potential are prematurely ended. In the situation with Maria, the "perfect" confrontation might sound like this:

You: Maria, that joke you told made me uncomfortable. It sounded a little racist. I don't mean to be a drag, but I get a little sensitive around racial jokes. Can I ask if it was just a joke you heard somewhere or do you really feel that way?

Maria: I did hear that joke the other night on television. I found it funny and didn't particularly find it offensive. But now that we are talking about it, I see how it could be. I do not usually go around making offensive jokes about different people and I wouldn't want you to get that impression of me.

You: I'm really glad to hear that and I'm also glad I brought this up because I understand you better now.

Maria: I'm really sorry that I offended you. I really didn't mean anything by it. And I'm glad you said something, too.

Maybe the average confrontation between people doesn't go this smoothly and maturely, but the above conversation is possible. A more common, but less constructive, confrontation might sound something like this:

You: I really hate ethnic or racial jokes. They bother me. Are you racist or something?

Maria: I am not a racist. It was a joke. I was trying to make you laugh and lighten up the atmosphere. I can't help it if you don't have a sense of humor.

You: Well, it didn't work on me because I don't find those jokes funny.

Maria: O.K., I will be more careful when choosing jokes to tell you. I didn't realize that you are so overly sensitive.

This confrontation includes important elements in it. You showed your feelings, told what you didn't like and asked a question for clarification. Maria answered the question, explained herself, and made a correction in her behavior. But the tone of the conversation was angry, insensitive and accusatory. It created an atmosphere that clarified superficial aspects of the issue, not the deeper ones. Both people probably did not feel particularly closer to each other after it.

A SIMPLE FORMULA FOR ASSERTIVENESS

In all areas of assertiveness, it is important to find your own words and style to express yourself. But with confrontation, a positive outcome is more likely if the conversation is about:

◊   feelings
◊   reasons for those feelings
◊   a request for what you want
◊   an interest in understanding the other person's position

ROOT CAUSES OF UNASSERTIVENESS

Unassertiveness can be a painful behavior to endure and a difficult one to overcome. We have all suffered from it at one time or another. We can relate to being frozen in fear, which keeps us from speaking up at a meeting or being too uncomfortable to talk to someone we are attracted to. The reasons for this problem differ from person to person.

Common causes for unassertiveness are:

1. modeling of your family
2. shyness or fear of rejection and abandonment
3. lack of knowing yourself in an intimate way
4. lack of knowledge about assertive skills

UNASSERTIVENESS PARENTAL MODELING

If your parents were unassertive people, it is possible that you follow their example. It's all you know. You may have known your mother wanted to ask your dad to help her with the dishes, but didn't ask. She may have made excuses about his tiredness or his not liking to wash dishes, but the bottom line was she didn't stand up to him and ask for what *she* wanted or needed.

Your dad may have wanted your mom to work instead of being a full-time mother and housewife. He may have felt a lot of financial stress and needed the help. He may not have asked her out of guilt or embarrassment. But *his* unassertiveness may have penetrated *your* psyche, rendering you helpless to ask for help.

HOW TO REVERSE THE MODELING AND BECOME MORE ASSERTIVE

1. Tell yourself it is O.K. not to be like your parents. They did the best they could. It's O.K. to be more assertive about what you want. You needn't feel guilty about being different from your parents.

2. Remind yourself of the negative results of your parents unassertiveness; i.e., they often looked worried, tired, angry or sad.

3. Take courses, go to counseling or read books that teach techniques for overcoming the fear of expressing yourself.

SHYNESS, FEAR OF REJECTION & ABANDONMENT

Shyness means to be "retiring or easily frightened away." It refers to interpersonal emotional fear. Shy people avoid new situations where they fear they might be hurt or embarrassed in some way. At the core of shyness is low self-esteem and lack of the personal empowerment to be assertive. Along with this goes the fear of not being good enough for anyone to love you and stay with you.

THE DREADED SINGLES DANCE AND SHYNESS

A singles dance is the classic place where shyness rules, and fear of rejection is the most common obsession on the dance floor. There you are, with your great hairdo and jeans that fit just right. You are surrounded by single people who seem to have noticed you. If you're shy, you divert your eyes away from their glance, you do not smile back or you begin to worry that you hair is sticking up or you need to blow your nose. Why are you acting this way? You *knew* you looked fine, before you left home. You are there to meet people, so what is the problem? You are scared, you feel inadequate and believe that rejection is imminent.

You may have inherited your shyness or possibly some trauma occurred in your life that caused you to fear personal harm in some way from relationships. The shy person at a singles dance probably puts in more time in the restroom than a person with Montezuma's Revenge. Shyness ruins the chance for many relationships to even begin.

OVERCOMING SHYNESS, FEAR OF REJECTION AND ABANDONMENT

1. Take steps to build your self-esteem (see suggestions in Chapter One).
2. Practicing assertiveness with people you trust will help you become more comfortable with the new behavior.
3. Learn stress-management techniques (as a way of managing the anxiety that accompanies shyness), breathing techniques, yoga, exercise, developing new

thinking styles, and taking good care of yourself
physically and mentally.

4. Get to the root of what you are really afraid of. (Get
professional help, if necessary, to overcome this fear
permanently.)

The good news about shyness, fear of rejection and fear of
abandonment is that you can free yourself of these traits that
inhibit you and you can learn to enjoy relationships. Such traits do
not have to remain permanent fixtures in your life, like birthmarks,
tattoos or taxes.

LEARNING ABOUT YOURSELF

Dating and relationship success require that the people
involved know themselves. How can you be comfortable with
being assertive when you are confused or indifferent about what
you want and how you feel? Information about yourself, whether
it is of major or minor importance, should be understood by you.
Look at what happens when someone tries to get to know you and
encourages you to reveal yourself—and you look like a deer
caught in the headlights:

Bob: (driving in the car with Debra)
        What movie would you like to see?

Debra: I don't know.

Bob: What kind of movie is your favorite?

Debra: I couldn't say what my favorite type is. I like many
        different kinds.

Bob: O.K. if I choose then?

Debra: Sure.

Bob: (Bob and Debra sitting in the theater; Debra with her head
        down and eyes closed)
        Are you all right?

Debra: Yes, I feel tired. I don't like this movie.

Bob: Is it upsetting you or boring you?

Debra: I'm not sure why I don't like it.

Debra is unable to give one answer that reflects any insight
into herself. She is giving Bob no help in understanding her. Her
lack of self-knowledge has led to unassertiveness. Bob chose an

action movie that is violent. Debra has always avoided movies with violence. But she has never taken the time to analyze and understand why. When Bob asks her for her preference, she does not have a deep enough understanding about herself to assertively tell Bob what she prefers and doesn't prefer. The result is that she is uncomfortable, he is uncomfortable, neither is having fun and he ultimately feels guilty that he suggested this movie. Wouldn't you prefer staying home and rearranging your sock drawer than going on a date like this?

GET TO KNOW YOURSELF

1. Spend time learning about who you were as a child and adolescent. What you learn may shed light on who you are today. (Talk to parents, look at old photographs, talk to other family members.)

2. Go into counseling. Set a goal of analyzing and understanding your likes, dislikes and fears.

3. Pay attention to the items you buy, the places you go and what you spend time thinking about.

You will be more successful at choosing a compatible partner if you know yourself better. It would be like choosing a vacation destination without knowing what kind of trip you are in the mood for. You would not want to end up at the Grand Canyon and experience cravings for French food and the theater. And you would not want to end up with Mr. or Mrs. Constant Business Traveler if you really want to be with Mr. or Mrs. Homebody. If you know yourself intimately, you can avoid such experiences.

THE GOAL OF ASSERTIVENESS

Let us first describe what the goal of assertiveness is *not*. It is not a manipulative technique that gives you control over other people. It is not a guarantee that you will win or get your way. Assertiveness *is* a technique that guarantees clarity for those around you regarding who you are, how you feel, what you want and how you think.

Becoming skilled at assertiveness does not guarantee that people will listen to you, respect you or change themselves or their ideas in any way. Appropriate assertiveness *will* increase the odds of achieving the positive results that you wish for. If you ask your boss for a raise and tell him why you think you deserve it, there is more of a chance that you will get it than if you just passively sulk on payday or give him scowling looks.

For example:

You: Jerry, I feel I have been doing very well in my job and in helping to enhance the company's bottom line. I've been here one year and would like to discuss increasing my salary. When do you have time to meet with me?

Boss: You are doing a great job, but I'm not sure what I can do for you regarding a raise. Let's meet tomorrow and discuss your performance and see what the options are. I will do what I can to help.

The above exchange represents an assertive approach to a supervisor and a reasonable answer from an open, fair and responsive boss. But you could have spoken just as assertively with a difficult boss and experienced a very different result:

You: Jerry, I feel I have been doing very well in my job and in helping to enhance the company's bottom line. I've been here one year and would like to discuss increasing my salary. When do you have time to meet with me?

Boss: I am too busy to discuss raises at this time, but keep up the good work.

Or:

Your performance has been O.K., but it could improve. I'll let you know when I am considering you for a raise.

These responses are not positive and ignore the credibility of your very appropriate assertion. Don't let a bad result deter you from continuing to be assertive. If you speak up, at least there is a chance of being heard and getting what you want.

SUMMARY

Being assertive helps you get your needs met. It helps you grow, change and learn to know yourself. It raises your self-esteem and makes you feel and *become* more powerful in your life. It helps you *win* at times, or at least increase your control in situations. It allows you to influence people and situations. It helps you become better known by others. It builds self-respect and the respect of others for you. Despite the fact that it can be difficult to do at times, it is clear what an important role assertiveness can play in your life.

If you're tired of eating cold food in restaurants because you're afraid to send it back, or angry for letting your tailor think it is acceptable that he hemmed your pants the perfect length for walking in a flood, then start speaking up for yourself. We know it is hard to be assertive, but we encourage you to push through the discomfort and *do it.*

If, in your single life, you are tired of suffering through "the kiss from hell" or overwhelmed with boredom because you allow your date to corner you in conversations about people you have never met, you must find the voice inside you that can say, "No, thank you," "Please stop," "Excuse me" or "Good-bye!"

HEALTHY DATING RULE #8

Express your thoughts and feelings consistently. Show equal respect and consideration for yourself and others in the way you communicate.

CHAPTER NINE

Foolish Dating Mistake # 9

·-∽◯∽

YOUR COMMUNICATION SKILLS ARE INADEQUATE OR INAPPROPRIATE

QUIZ:

You are a poor communicator because…

1. "I don't know" and "Maybe" are the only words in your vocabulary.

2. you think quality conversation is possible while simultaneously surfing the net and cooking your dinner.

3. you believe people should be able to read your mind.

We know that you're tired of hearing about "communication skills" from therapists. Every talk show has a guest therapist who listens to the most ridiculous problems and then tells people all they need to do is communicate more effectively.

If your behavior is out of control, communication is a back-burner issue. If you feel that your life is basically in good order, then it makes sense to take a look at whether or not you are able to communicate in a way that is clear and interesting and that you are not making Foolish Dating Mistake #9.

FOUR MAJOR COMMUNICATION MISTAKES

1. You are arrogant and a know-it-all.
2. You discuss your ex too much with dates.
3. You are nosy.
4. You are a poor conversationalist.

1–YOU ARE ARROGANT & A KNOW-IT-ALL

Ask yourself if you have ever had a discussion to the death. Also, ask yourself if you have ever been wrong. If you have frequent arguments and are never wrong, you are a "know-it-all." Let us be the latest to tell you that your style of communication is very annoying. You may see yourself as the person most designated to instruct or inform others, but it's time to understand that that is *not* your job. Communication is a two-way street between people, otherwise it is called a lecture. It is possible that you are very bright and well-versed on many subjects; even so, you don't know everything.

When on a date, it is important to search for things that you have in common and create a forum for discussion. If you are the ultimate authority on everything, you limit the discussion to what *you* think and feel. Friends have told us that their bossy dates act as if they know more about our friends' jobs than our friends do.

Example:

Jose: Yes. I'm a lawyer. I've always enjoyed standing up for others— law school was a dream of mine. It's been ten years now since I began practicing.

Ann: (the know-it-all)
Oh, well, I'm a florist. But one time I had to go to court over a vendor who had worked with us and didn't pay his bill. I learned as much as any lawyer on that case and now I advise all of my friends when it comes to legal things. I was just explaining to my girlfriend that she should pack up her tenant's things and change all the locks and get rid of him

because he was a week late on the rent. He can just find his stuff outside or stolen if he's going to be late.

Jose: Well, you might tell her to be careful because tenants have certain rights the landlord must observe in order to stay within the law of eviction.

Ann: No, no. I gave her good advice, believe me. My Uncle Ned went through the same thing. Maybe you didn't study this in law school. I am very sure that I gave good advice.

Ann needs to get a grip and let her date, the lawyer, give his opinion on the situation. Even if Ann feels she has a point, it is common goodwill to allow and encourage your date to speak his or her mind without dominating the whole conversation. You could be in Ann's situation and still have a good conversation:

Jose: You might want to be careful about the advice you gave your friend because tenants have certain rights.

Ann: Well, I thought that I gave great advice, but why? What do you mean?

Jose: Well...
(now Jose gets a chance to show a little expertise and Ann may take his advice or not, but now at least Ann is having a conversation instead of being a know-it-all.)

Ann: That's pretty interesting. Thanks, but I think she's going to go this way, but I'll let you know how it turns out.

Jose: O.K., great.

Being full of yourself and acting like you have some knowledge about every subject makes you boring and uninteresting. People want to know that *they* can add something to the conversation without you topping it or correcting it. Argumentative people often feel very insecure or unintelligent and are constantly trying to look smart and well-informed. Truly smart people let conversations flow, with each person putting their opinion in the pot for a soft, relaxing discussion. You must ask yourself if you always want to be right or do you always want to have a good relationship? You can't have both.

2–YOU DISCUSS YOUR EX-GIRLFRIEND/BOYFRIEND OR HUSBAND/WIFE

Will you allow us to save some time and sum this up? *Don't Do It!* Discussing your former relationships of whatever kind is the kiss of death on a date. When asked about past relationships, please keep in mind that dates do not want or cannot handle the truth in all its glory and in marathon detail. *Don't Do It!* Until you are heavily involved, the following are examples of how to answer questions about an ex:

1. We went our separate ways when we stopped working together. At that point, it just didn't seem to be the same.

2. We mutually agreed that we didn't bring out the best in each other.

3. It was a difficult situation from the start since he had four young children.

4. We were both at very vulnerable places in our lives and it wasn't a good time for a relationship for us.

5. The more we got to know each other, the more we realized we were too different

...and other equally vague but honest answers. Details and total honesty are for long-term relationships *only*. This is such an easy dating mistake to make because it feels intimate and you know the subject matter well. But we guarantee that 9.9 times out of 10, you will be in error when talking about an ex on a date. Even if your date asks about your ex and goes on and on about his/her own, committing this particular foolish dating mistake will make you appear stuck and vulnerable. You may not feel that way inside, but it will come across like that.

EXAMPLE OF SOUNDING STUCK AND VULNERABLE

Jessica: So have you been in many long-term relationships?

Rod: Well, yes. I broke up with my girlfriend of five years about two years ago. She was a very nice lady and we thought of getting married. But her dad was an alcoholic and that really messed up her whole life. Her mom never did anything to protect her either. There was a lot of violence and scary stuff.

Her dad ended up cheating on her mom and everyone knew it. This made Angela a very jealous person...

O.K. Rod, enough! All Rod had to say to answer the question was that he had a girlfriend for five years until two years ago. If asked why it didn't work out, he could have said, "I felt that she had some serious issues from her violent childhood to work out before she could go on to a great relationship." That's it; that's enough information for now.

Naturally, bringing up the ex when you haven't been asked about him or her and talking on and on about what a worthless piece of dirt your ex is, is the double kiss of dating death. Did we mention...*Don't Do It!*?

3–YOU ARE NOSY

We know why this is such a common communication mistake. You are a) anxious to find out everything about your date in order to decide whether you like him/her or not; b) you want to keep the attention off yourself, so you keep asking questions; or c) you have no life and you are nosy! Nosy conversations sound like this:

Valerie: So where do you live?

Jack: I live in Brentwood in a condo by Chase Street. It's nice, I like it there. Where do you live?

Valerie: I live in Santa Monica, not too far from you. I have a house close to 26th Street and Wilshire.

Jack: When did you buy it?

Valerie: Five years ago.

Jack: (nosy question)
          How much did you pay?

Valerie: I thought I paid a pretty fair market price.

Jack: (off the nosy meter)
          Oh, Yeah? How much? How much are your house payments?

Valerie: Well, I seem to meet them each month and that's what's important.

Jack: Does someone help you do that?

Bye, bye Jack. He completely missed how Valerie was answering in a polite but firm way in order to let him know that he was asking about something beyond his business. Valerie wasn't being evasive, Jack was being nosy. Some people seem to feel that their dates should be willing to answer *any* question, no matter how personal and how little is known about them, or they are not open and honest. This is not true.

There is such a thing as conversation boundaries that need to be respected, especially in the beginning. Do not continue to pry if you notice that your questions are not being answered directly about matters that have nothing to do with you. For example, why they left their religion or how much money they make is not essential for you to know right away and they are out-of-bounds questions. It is a different matter (and not nosy), however, to ask and expect a direct response to, "Are you married?"

Why they brought their pet yak along on the date is also an appropriate and necessary question having to do with you. Otherwise, stay away from deeply personal questions at the beginning and give yourself the chance to get to know the person over time.

WHY ARE PEOPLE NOSY?

One way people try to keep the heat and the conversation off themselves is by asking questions of the other person. A lot of people are interested in getting to know their date, but prefer to remain mysterious themselves. It is time to get over this because it is a setup for a bad start. Ask yourself why you need to hide on a date. What are you hiding? Unless you are on an active CIA case, you are being a poor date by not sharing information about yourself. Being elusive and mysterious is only excusable when you're a teenager. Get in there and participate.

Sometimes people come from nosy families. If you do, then you are accustomed to having your business considered to be everyone's business and you may think that's normal. The truth is that it represents overfamiliarity. Part of being polite is to respect other people's privacy and boundaries.

4–YOU ARE A POOR CONVERSATIONALIST

Raise your right hand and repeat after us:

I _____ (state your name), do solemnly promise to prepare and execute decent and lively conversation when on dates. Further, I _____ will not take this promise lightly, since I realize that it is my duty as a dater to uphold this oath. Also, I will not do anything else to distract me while talking on the phone to my date, nor will I do anything else that will generally make me boring or boorish. I will pay careful attention to social cues so that I am not "disconnected" while on a date.

You may lower you right hand and congratulate yourself on being of sound dating capacity as you carry out these solemnly made promises.

Let's look at them more closely.

I WILL NOT DO ANYTHING ELSE WHILE TALKING ON THE PHONE

Yes, talking is the primary activity when you're on the phone, and no matter how clever you believe yourself to be, it does not leave room for working on the computer, surfing the net, watching TV (even with the sound off), making a grocery list, paying bills, washing dishes, etc.

If you're a good conversationalist, you will focus on the other person, whether talking on the phone or in a face-to-face conversation. It is very rude to be doing something else simultaneously and it diminishes your ability to keep up your end in a lively and meaningful way.

In addition, the other person feels bad when he or she hears you clicking on your keyboard. The message is being conveyed that he or she is not important enough to command your attention. If you feel that way, either you shouldn't go out with him/her or you should shorten your phone conversations and spend in-person time together to see if he/she is more compelling than by phone. Or, consider whether *you* are the reason for the mediocre conversation.

On Being A Bore

Being a conversational bore means that you show up for a date without a single thought of what you like to talk about that is interesting to most people. Everyone should have a story or topic to turn to if things slow down. Most people would enjoy a good travel story or something that happened that had a fun twist at the end, or any light and humorous adventure or situation that you have had or have heard about. In addition, stay away from long stories without humor or about people your date doesn't know.

If you are very shy or you simply run out of things to say, plan the kind of date that has built-in topics. A controversial subject based on a movie or a play will stimulate discussion afterward.

Keep up with current events and work on generating topics. You might want to explore whether your date is interested in music, TV, talk radio or books that you love.

Watch For Those Social Cues!

If you are in the middle of a long story and notice that your date has nodded off face-first into the angel-hair pasta, you are being boring and missing the obvious cues. Glassy eyes, lots of fidgeting and staring at a watch can signal that you have gone on too long. Never talk for five minutes or more without a word from your date. When people are enjoying a good conversation, they usually look lively, with a wide-open, attentive expression.

Do not be one of those people who fail to notice they have trapped someone in a dull conversation, as is evident by the other person's glazed, emotionless expression. Be aware of others' responses and occasionally turn the conversation around by using a question to engage your date.

STAYING CONNECTED TO THE CONVERSATION

Those who are skilled at conversation build on what others say. This is highly effective. If they are talking about something that happened to them, you respond appropriately with, "Oh, really?" or "How funny!" or "Then what happened?" and tell a similar story if you have one. That shows the person that you were listening with enthusiasm and have something to share as well. If your date is talking about his or her grandmother, comment first on what was said and then when there is a pause, add a little about your grandparent. This makes you a connected date and helps to bring out what the two of you have in common.

Great communication requires the ability to listen actively. This means that you are paying attention along the way and adding something that you know or believe—when appropriate. Good communicators leave room for others to fill in their stories as well. Humor and honesty are the best tools when used with some common sense. You are truly doing it right together when you see the conversation flow with an exchange of ideas and no underlying antagonism.

Great communication makes for a great date experience. Many report that even though they were not initially attracted to their date, they changed their mind completely after talking with them throughout the evening. It is not a bad idea to ask those whom you trust to give you tips on what your communications strengths and weaknesses are. Use those strengths and improve upon the weak areas. It is definitely worth it.

SUMMARY

Think about your most recent first or second dates and try to remember if you added to the conversation and the success of the date. Were you able to listen, add interesting notes to the topics and generate some of your own topics? Were you able to do this without talk of an ex or by being too nosy with highly personal questions? Good conversation on your part can only bring out the best in your date. If your date's best stories click with you, then you have the basis of a relationship in which you can really talk to the person and be heard and be interested enough to attentively listen. These skills truly deepen the connection between two people.

HEALTHY DATING RULE #9

Contribute your share to good conversation when on a date, don't forget to listen with your full attention, and be respectful of your date's right to privacy and boundaries.

CHAPTER TEN

Foolish Dating Mistake #10

·⟿∞⟿·

YOU USE POOR JUDGMENT

QUIZ:

Poor judgment is:

1. dating someone who is married.
2. dating someone who makes your toes tingle but your mind go numb.
3. showing up for a date in pajamas.

WHAT IS GOOD JUDGMENT, ANYWAY?

Good judgment is the ability to think through choices and make a *healthy* decision or form a wise opinion. Being open to relationships with many different types of people is great if you know when it is time either to be vulnerable to a good situation or close the door on a bad situation.

Constant decision-making based on good judgment is necessary for successful relationships. Good judgment is based on asking yourself these questions:

◊ Am I ready and emotionally healthy enough for a relationship?

◊ Is the person I am attracted to emotionally healthy and available?

◊   Do I want to make a commitment or just date and have a good time?

◊   Do I want to eat Chinese food, catch a movie, or have sex?

To answer these questions wisely, you first have to think about what you want. A lover? A life partner? A friend? A companion to spend holidays with? A soul mate?

To make the right decision for ourselves, we have to know what the possible outcomes are and how we feel about each possible outcome. For example, one outcome might be that you end up in an exclusive relationship with someone. Then you must ask yourself how you *feel* about being in that exclusive relationship. If your desire for that outcome is high, the situation looks healthy and the desired outcome is a realistic possibility, it would be a good judgment call to go for it.

WHY IS GOOD JUDGMENT SO IMPORTANT?

The idea behind using good judgment is to prevent disaster. Most single people know that dating and relationship disasters often are more emotionally difficult to deal with than other forms of disaster. This is because with a natural disaster we can blame a force other than ourselves. With a relationship disaster, at some point you must accept blame for its disastrous outcome. It is not nature's fault that you keep dating that person who thinks joking about the space between your front teeth is funny. And why is doing this indicative of using poor judgment? Because you cannot possibly like the outcome of the date and you cannot possibly feel good about it. So how could dating this person be a good judgment call? It cannot be.

Good judgment in this situation would sound like this:

I'm never going out with that person again. I felt very uncomfortable with her sense of humor. She is rude.

or

I'm going to have to tell this woman that her joking about my teeth offends me and that if she doesn't stop it, I have no reason to continue seeing her.

These statements exhibit good judgment because they show that you know what you want and are willing to take action to get it. Good judgment is like an emotional insurance policy. It protects you from decisions that lead to involvement with people who are going to hurt you. Good judgment kicks in—even when emotions are running high. It urges you to move close to a good relationship, possibly even when you're terrified, and to move away from a poor relationship even when you feel you're madly in love.

Having good judgment in relationships requires that you:

◊　know yourself (your feelings, values, goals)

◊　know what you want in a partner

◊　feel good about yourself and communicate your likes and dislikes

◊　take good care of yourself, emotionally, physically and financially

◊　be mature

When you disregard these aspects of yourself and choose to get involved with a person based only on a whim or a feeling, you are setting yourself up to fail. It is important that you possess these traits so you can intelligently assess the situation you're in or about to be in. If you have not acquired these five necessary qualities, then perhaps you are presently unavailable for a good relationship.

Instead of searching for the perfect partner and being disappointed, you can spend time on yourself and your reasons for wanting a healthy relationship. This time, when productively spent, also will make it easier for you to notice when someone else is ready to be involved.

Having poor judgment with relationships means that you:

◊　pursue (or stay with) someone when *you* are not available

◊　pursue (or stay with) someone when *they* are not available

◊　pursue (or stay with) someone who is inappropriate for you

HOW TO DEVELOP GOOD JUDGMENT

When it comes to making good connections, wanting to be ready isn't enough. Without the aforementioned five traits, you are vulnerable to abuse, dependency and failure in your personal relationships. Also, when a relationship ends, it is the people who lack these things who fall apart and are unable to function normally. This is because when their relationship ends, they feel they have lost the most vital part of themselves and they feel a loss of hope for all future happiness.

Knowing yourself in a deep and accurate way means understanding how you think and feel about the things that matter most to you.

Establishing a clear set of values and committing to live by them is an integral part of personal identity. If you enter into a relationship while unclear about your values and beliefs, you run the risk of losing your identity in that relationship. You also run the risk of becoming frustrated, unfulfilled and angry. It is like eating a salad when you really want a steak. If you have made the wrong choice, you continue to yearn for something else. But in a relationship, the stakes are higher than in the choice of a meal. Feelings and self-esteem are at risk. Insufficient self-awareness makes us vulnerable to being used, manipulated or hurt. Skilled manipulators can sense a lack of identity—and when they do, they use that vulnerability for their own ends. You are not ready for a relationship if you can be controlled in this way.

Pursuing interests is another important part of a strong identity. It can be a factor in establishing compatibility with someone. It also helps keep us independent. If a relationship does not work out, continuing to enjoy your interests keeps you busy and reinforces your identity as separate from your newly ended relationship.

How well we know ourselves also affects the kinds of judgments we make. If we guess at what we want and we're wrong, we repeat negative patterns. If we are confused or unfocused about what we want, we are unable to clearly communicate "Yes" or "No" to simple questions or requests. This communication problem can be disastrous for the beginning stages of a relationship.

Being aware of your feelings and beliefs protects you from making the wrong decisions. People who say "Yes" when "No" would be more appropriate for them may end up in situations they wish they had never been in. People who know themselves say "Yes" when it is right and "No" when it is wrong. Have you ever been in a situation where saying "Yes" got you stuck on a boring date or in a dangerous situation? Keep in mind that you have the power to avoid having that happen to you.

HOW TO DEVELOP A DEEPER LEVEL OF SELF-AWARENESS

1. Spend quality time alone.
2. Observe and assess the choices you make for yourself by yourself; i.e., without the input and influence of others.
3. Observe how you *feel* about the choices you make.
4. Make a commitment to yourself to pursue the activities you enjoy and feel positive about.
5. Make a commitment to yourself to avoid and dismiss the actions that you do not enjoy or that are negative for you.
6. Make a list of dreams and goals.

Knowing what you want and need from a partner means *to understand what type of person would be the most compatible with you.* Once you become aware of your deepest feelings and beliefs, you are on your way to being able to choose an appropriate person for yourself. This person should have the potential to fulfill you in significant areas such as communication, affection, goals and sex. These areas of a relationship are fulfilled when a high degree of compatibility exists. Need fulfillment in these areas creates a strong foundation to build on.

If you're fed up with relationship disappointment, ask yourself these two questions at the beginning and middle stages of any relationship:

1. What do I want from this person?
2. Does he or she have the capacity and the willingness to give it to me?

These simple questions indicate whether or not you will get what you want. Naturally, we all compromise, but it is unwise to do so with the core issues, such as communication, affection, goals, values, and sexual issues. For example, if a major goal of your life is to have children and the person you are getting serious with already has five children and has had a vasectomy or tubal ligation and thinks that more children would be a cruel twist of fate, you are investing in the wrong love stock. You cannot be fulfilled with this partner. When your most basic needs or goals do not match, it's time to leave.

It is extremely important to acknowledge our humanness and to expect our wants and needs to be important to persons we are involved with.

You Are Ready for a Relationship When You Can Say to Someone (at the appropriate point):

I know that I need you to ask me about my feelings and be outwardly demonstrative about how much you care about those feelings. I also want you to be willing and interested in helping me if I need or ask for it.

While those words may not be your exact sentiments or style of communication, you can find your own words to communicate your need to be cared for in a special way. A person who agrees to these requests and follows through with action is a good candidate for a relationship.

Getting into a relationship is as stressful as it is exciting. Being willing to talk about significant issues in an honest and positive way allows a person to get to know the "real" you. The "game-playing" style of dating can be bypassed if you can determine the level of compatibility in the relationship. After all, aren't you tired of wasting time?

Your ability to listen and reserve judgment until you get to know someone is crucial in the beginning stages of dating. Do you criticize differences between yourself and the other person? Do you mistrust? Do you see self-disclosures as unimportant? When we are afraid of intimacy, we look for excuses not to trust and not to take risks. One way of accomplishing this is to misinterpret what we're told and decide not to be vulnerable. But in doing this, the relationship loses the potential to grow. Risk-taking is part of being open. If you have old hurts that keep you closed, you must find a way to react differently to your past. This new way of thinking and being must allow you to believe that there are people who can be trusted and that being vulnerable again will lead to more fulfillment than remaining closed to feelings will. *Active, nonjudgmental listening creates an atmosphere of friendliness and trust. Such an atmosphere is fertile ground for intimacy.*

FEELING GOOD ABOUT YOURSELF & YOUR LIFE

Happy people generally like themselves. They feel positive about the things they like. They can tolerate hearing "No" without getting upset. In a healthy relationship, each person is insightful and accepting of themselves. They usually are able to enjoy life and keep a positive outlook because their self-esteem allows them to feel worthy of that happy feeling. To possess self-esteem means that we feel confident in our ability to think, judge and act in a reasonable and effective manner. People who like themselves treat themselves and others with respect and caring. They tend to be positive, creative and giving. A relationship between two people who like themselves has great potential for a successful outcome. Conversely, it is nearly impossible to love people who do not love themselves.

STEPS NECESSARY TO RAISE YOUR SELF-ESTEEM

◊   Set goals and work toward them
◊   Surround yourself with positive people
◊   Stop addictive, compulsive behaviors
◊   Pamper yourself
◊   Continue to learn new skills or strengthen existing ones

◊   Make your work life as fulfilling as possible
◊   Talk to yourself in positive terms—stop the habit of negative self-talk

TAKE CARE OF YOURSELF PHYSICALLY & EMOTIONALLY

Relationships can be as difficult as they are exciting and fulfilling. You have to be up for the challenges as well as the rewards. To be ready, you must feel good physically and emotionally.

Feeling good physically requires:
◊   Getting sufficient sleep
◊   Getting sufficient exercise
◊   Eating well
◊   Getting medical attention as needed
◊   Taking pride in your appearance
◊   Getting sufficient relaxation and recreation

Not attending to any one of these self-care areas can contribute to lack of energy, attractiveness and consciousness, which make it difficult to be in a healthy relationship.

Too many people use alcohol and drugs to help them deal with low self-esteem or shyness. Use of chemicals eventually will cause severe deterioration in physical and mental well-being. No healthy person wants to be around people who are destroying themselves. It's not fun or attractive and precludes real intimacy.

Feeling good emotionally includes:
◊   Having and maintaining self-esteem
◊   Resolving emotional issues from the past
◊   Communicating feelings, wants and needs
◊   Fulfilling dreams and desires
◊   Being assertive
◊   Attaining independence

When we feel good emotionally, we're able to enjoy dating and having relationships. We can be creative, positive, giving and grateful when our minds are nurtured. Neglect in this area can lead to serious problems, such as depression and anxiety. For example, the person who has not resolved problems from the past can bring those negative feelings and beliefs into new relationships. Judgment is impaired when we confuse issues from the past with issues in the present.

Listen to Jeff talking to his new love interest:

Jeff: Mary, you said you were going to call last night and you didn't. I take that to mean you can't be trusted at all.

Mary: Jeff, I think I told you I would try to call. I got home very late and did not want to wake you up. I told you I might have to work late—and I did.

Jeff: You still should have called. You should have made me more important than work.

Mary: You are very important to me, Jeff. Why are you so hurt and suspicious about my not calling? Everything has been going so well between us—until this!

Jeff: You are right, things have gone well. But this proves it was only a matter of time before something would happen to break my trust.

Mary: I think you are overreacting. In fact, it sounds like you have been hurt very badly in the past.

We'll bet you can guess what is happening with Jeff. Mary is right. He has been hurt. He is mistrusting and interprets situations in a negative way. He apparently really likes Mary and wants her to like him. But because he has not healed from some past rejection or trauma, he brings those negative emotions to his relationship with Mary.

A major key to staying healthy is to be open to experience all feelings as they occur and to be willing to deal with them. "Dealing with" means talking about them, writing about them, accepting them as valid or getting counseling to sort through them. With awareness and openness to our feelings, emotional health is attainable. It is in this open and healthy emotional state that we attract healthy partners. Without this sound emotional state, chaos and drama can dominate and destroy your romantic relationships.

SET HIGH STANDARDS FOR CONSISTENT EMOTIONAL HAPPINESS BETWEEN YOU & YOUR PARTNER

All relationships have problems, but chronic emotional distress that feels unending should not be tolerated. You must care about yourself enough to expect to be happy with someone. Being happy means feeling thankful to be alive, looking forward to your life on a daily basis, and experiencing love and acceptance in your life from your intimate relationships.

BEING MATURE

Being mature simply means "being of your age." What does this really mean when we are talking about relationships? It means not getting involved in situations that you are emotionally unprepared for due to lack of experience or developmental awareness. Maturity contributes to understanding what a relationship really involves. Mature people expect ups and downs to occur in a relationship. They know that no one person or situation is perfect. They understand the need for constant communication involving negotiating and compromising. They know that disappointment in some form is inevitable and normal; no *one* person can fulfill *all* of your needs all of the time. Immature persons are shocked and devastated by such disappointments. They think love conquers all problems. They think everything should feel easy if it is right. They do not fully communicate but, instead, project and fantasize.

Take a woman in her twenties who gets involved with a man in his forties. She has been sheltered by her family. He is worldly, experienced and confident. She thinks their romance will lead to marriage. She starts making assumptions and plans related to a permanent future. He reacts with anger at her assumptions. She is devastated and confused. She thought she had read things accurately. He breaks up with her. He didn't realize she was so "young" and would jump to conclusions about their relationship. He was enjoying himself, but without thoughts of commitment. He wanted to have fun, without any ties. Each of them made a poor judgment call when they decided to get involved.

At any age we can think and act immaturely and, as a result, destroy a relationship and cause ourselves emotional distress. Being intellectually and emotionally mature helps us see a relationship for what it is. It helps us function appropriately in the relationship or helps us make the right decision about whether to stay or to leave.

Maturity is a state of mind that is achieved by age and/or experience. But you must allow yourself the benefit of this age and experience by examining the events that happen to you and how you react to them. Analyzing helps us learn from our experience and become mature.

THE KEY TO GOOD JUDGMENT

The key to good judgment is to understand the reality of the situation, the possible outcomes of that situation and how you feel about those outcomes.

Judgments are formed by what we are taught, what we see done or by the desperation we may feel about wanting something to happen for us in our lives—such as finding a partner. This desperation can cause us to be confused and unclear about what we should do or how we feel. Each of the other foolish dating mistakes involves the use of poor judgment.

MISTAKE #1—YOU GIVE TOO MUCH TOO SOON

The faulty judgment here is that too much too soon will make things go faster, which will result in a good ending. This is about as true as saying that eating a big Italian meal in five minutes (cappuccino and dessert included) will make it taste better and digest more quickly. This makes no sense and neither does trying to fall in love with someone on your first date. Doing either one could give you monumental heartburn.

To eliminate the use of poor judgment in the areas of giving too much too soon, remember to:

1. Get to know the person before you forge ahead into the pursuit of ecstasy.

2. Protect yourself by setting limits for the other person regarding their treatment of you.

3. Give when it is appropriate and as a way to communicate feelings (not as an attempt to manipulate another person or to cover up your insecurities).

4. If someone you are dating descends upon your life like an avalanche, get out of the way and let him/her continue downhill—after making it clear that getting snowed under by too much emotion is not what you're after.

MISTAKE #2–YOU HOLD BACK UNTIL IT'S TOO LATE

Many people hold back from giving in relationships for emotional reasons such as fear of rejection, fear of intimacy, or past unhealed resentments and hurt. Others hold back because they decide that this behavior creates mystery and chemistry in their relationships. Withholding something good from someone and expecting them to stay open and positive toward you is immature thinking. Mature people are not amused by stinginess. They find generosity in the person they are dating fun and enjoyable—when it is appropriately expressed.

Good judgment about how much to give involves understanding what stage your relationship is in. It involves knowing how you feel about people and knowing what you want from them in a relationship. You use poor judgment when you dole out crumbs to a partner after a long period of being together. If that partner has any self-esteem, he or she will get rid of you as quickly as one would a peddler at the front door.

Good judgment regarding generosity involves:

1. understanding what level of giving is appropriate at each stage of a relationship

2. realizing that giving is a crucial part of developing intimacy

3. communicating and staying aware of your feelings

MISTAKE #3—YOU FOCUS TOO MUCH ON PHYSICAL CHEMISTRY

If you are guilty of this, your judgment says (a) physical attraction is the most important aspect to consider in your relationship; (b) if physical appearance changes, the relationship is threatened; (c) you never look quite good enough to get close to someone.

Poor judgment in this area of dating kills a good relationship. When you are too busy looking at a person's body, you are too distracted to appreciate his/her mind and spirit. When you get addicted to the mirror, constantly checking yourself out for any imperfection you may have, you never feel good enough to date. Deciding that physical appearance is the most important aspect of a relationship will keep you feeling down on yourself and critical of others.

Solution: To counteract these poor judgment calls, it is essential that you:

1. remain open to experiencing many different kinds of people

2. stop staring at yourself in any shiny surface

3. experiment with changes in your appearance and have fun with it

4. take the time to get to know your date on a deeper personal level

MISTAKE #4—YOU LACK A DATING SENSE OF HUMOR

Getting to know someone requires that you not take yourself too seriously and that you remain open to playfulness. Making a serious commitment isn't humorous, but the dating stage goes much more smoothly if you reveal your sense of humor. As always, balance or moderation is the key. Some people use humor to hide their insecurities; as a result they act like stand-up comedians or play dodge ball with every topic by laughing them off. Others take themselves so seriously that any attempt at humor by the date is seen as an attack. Holding back the light side when dating is an especially poor judgment call.

Good judgment regarding humor requires:

1. a willingness to laugh at yourself (unless it truly is a hurtful situation)

2. staying available when a more serious tone is appropriate and not hiding behind a joke to avoid discomfort

3. not using "humor" to hurt others

MISTAKE #5–YOUR NEGATIVE HABITS OR ATTITUDES BLOCK COMMITMENT

Being too critical, inflexible, lazy, disrespectful, moody, sloppy, drunk or drugged pretty much sums up the areas in which we can make bad decisions and ruin a relationship. The scary fact is that many people who have these negative habits do not see themselves and their poor behavior clearly and, as a result, tend to blame their dates for the bad endings.

Good judgment regarding negative habits requires that you:

1. see your actions from the other person's point-of-view

2. listen and take seriously all constructive criticism

3. notice and emulate the thoughtfulness of others

MISTAKE #6–YOU RESIST COMMITMENT

Poor judgment frequently is used when people decide it is never the right time to commit. They often base their judgments on shallow concerns, such as "I'm not thin enough or rich enough or well-traveled enough to settle down."

We have even been told by clients that "My horoscope told me to wait" or "the Psychic Network suggested that I am not ready." We all have our beliefs, but judgments based on anything other than the reality of a situation and our feelings about that situation are usually way off the mark. It is like flipping a coin to help us decide whether or not to go to the doctor when we develop a 106-degree fever.

Good judgment regarding commitment issues requires that you:

1. know what your needs and wishes are

2. understand what will be expected of you in a committed relationship

3. keep an eye out for your pattern of resisting commitment and try to judge whether this person is bad for you to date or whether you are just running away

MISTAKE #7—YOU INTERVIEW FOR A SPOUSE

If you are in the "cut-to-the-chase" mode of dating and your goal is to find out in the first fifteen minutes whether your date is worth the investment, your judgment is going to be off. Instead of allowing necessary information to unfold in a more natural way, you make snap judgments. This represents poor judgment because you won't know enough about the "real" person before you act on your ill-gotten, instantly made assessment.

In order to use good judgment when seeking a compatible partner:

1. Don't interview—get rid of the pass/fail exam in your head.

2. Unless your date shows up with a monkey on his or her back, and introduces it as "my son," hold back on judgments based on first impressions or initial conversations.

MISTAKE #8—YOU ARE CONSISTENTLY UNASSERTIVE

It is indicative of poor judgment to be invisible in a relationship. Continuously holding back your opinions, desires, needs and points-of-view will always hurt you. Your judgment regarding being "present" in this way will teach people from the start whether or not they have to pay attention to you and respect you. Perhaps you wish to appear to be very easygoing, but having your personality disappear won't make for a good relationship.

Using good judgment by being assertive means:
1. not judging your own needs and opinions
2. making those needs and opinions known, as appropriate
3. keeping that balance between Wimpy and the Terminator

MISTAKE #9—INADEQUATE OR INAPPROPRIATE COMMUNICATION SKILLS

Faulty judgment would tell you that all of this "communication stuff" is something therapists invented to drive people crazy. You may tell yourself that if people are really in love, they know how they feel and if you have to talk about everything and have arguments, it is not meant to be. The opposite, of course, is true. Being present for your speaking part will move a relationship toward more health and intimacy.

To use good judgment in your communication skills, you must:
1. perceive conversation, communication and discussions as basic necessities for good relationships
2. search out ways in which you sabotage communication; for example, racheting up the volume on the big-screen TV to avoid hearing what is being said to you by your partner
3. avoid sudden slams when arguing—don't utter horrifying untruths just to put an end to the conversation or to score a "win"

WHEN IT IS DEFINITELY TIME TO LEAVE A RELATIONSHIP

Bad judgment is sometimes a result of habit. You've been with someone so long that you no longer know why you feel bad. Here is a quick list:

1. when the emotional, physical and/or financial costs outweigh the rewards
2. when abuse occurs
3. when your needs and wants are consistently ignored
4. when all communication has broken down and there is little or no hope of resolving it

IT IS POOR JUDGMENT TO STAY IN SUCH AN UNHEALTHY RELATIONSHIP

The inability to leave a dead relationship is a sign of dependency, fear and low self-esteem. In our need for someone, or in the haze of relationship addiction and the distortions that go with it, we are unable to be rational. We keep hoping for change when there is no reason to hope. We pretend that the situation is not so bad or even that it is all our fault. These are all attempts to avoid the feelings of being alone or feeling rejected.

An addictive relationship has very specific elements to it. People feel that they "need" to be together instead of "want" to be together. They are possessive, jealous, fearful and obsessive with each other. These relationships are filled with extremes, such as security and chaos, euphoria and despair. These behaviors and feelings destroy intimacy. It is time to leave a relationship when it becomes addictive.

WHEN THE EMOTIONAL, PHYSICAL AND/OR FINANCIAL COSTS OUTWEIGH THE REWARDS

The experience and evaluation of feelings is not an exact science. Sometimes it is hard to tell when the bad outweighs the good. You cannot add up numbers on a chart to help you know when it is time to call it quits with someone. This is why it is so important to stay aware of your feelings and take them seriously, especially the feelings that persist. For example, many people become master "minimizers" of their feelings. When we minimize we lose perspective on our own suffering. Minimizers tell themselves "Things aren't so bad" and "...it didn't hurt that much" rather than saying, "This is unacceptable and I'd better deal with what happened so it doesn't happen again."

For people who have to experience significant suffering before they can leave, here are some of the clear symptoms of extreme emotional distress:

1. Depression
2. Physical complaints
3. Continuous fear
4. Constant self-doubt
5. Frequent anger

When we're emotionally distressed, it becomes difficult to function. Because of a desire to have relationships work out, we may try to explain away our symptoms by blaming them on something else. But if your partner displays the following characteristics, you will experience emotional distress.

◊   Disloyalty
◊   Cruelty
◊   Withholding
◊   Impatience
◊   Lack of empathy
◊   Criticism
◊   Lack of affection

You may be thinking as you read this, "Well, of course, I would leave such a person." Really? Beware of rationalizations, which can sound like this:

"Maybe there is something bothering him and he can't help himself and he's taking it out on me because I'm safe" or "Maybe I have done something that I'm unaware of to cause this behavior" or "I am sure this attitude and behavior will pass in time—she's really a good person inside."

These serve as excuses not to leave the relationship. By avoiding the reality that abuse exists, we are placed at more risk for harm. Also, we only succeed in delaying the inevitable end of a bad relationship. Wouldn't it be better to have a relationship end before major trauma occurs?

How To Stop Rationalizing Away the Truth

1. Face your fears of being alone and get over them. Counseling may help.

2. Learn *how* to end a relationship. Explain what has not worked out for you, say good-bye and don't look back. It won't get better just because you *want* it to.

3. Instead of "explaining" to yourself why someone is acting a certain way, accept it as reality and *feel* it.

4. When you rationalize, ask yourself, "How do you know that statement is true? What are the facts that support it?"

5. Ask the person who is behaving badly, "Why?"

Learning *how* to leave a relationship will prepare you to be a better judge of *when* to leave it. Through the painful experience of the loss of a relationship (even a bad one) you will learn how to honor yourself and become attracted to a healthier person.

Summary

When you are healthy enough and the other person is healthy enough, and you're both using good judgment, *the sky is the limit for love and intimacy!*

Yet, you must accept that it takes hard work to accomplish this healthy readiness for a relationship. You also have to be willing to be patient and interested in really getting to know the person you are interested in. The better your initial choice of a partner, the better the odds that you will not fall into the trap of committing the other Foolish Dating Mistakes.

Healthy Dating Rule #10

Examine your ability to judge your choices in partners and your own behavior in those relationships.

ABOUT THE AUTHORS

Lila Gruzen holds a Ph.D. in Clinical Psychology and has been a licensed Marriage, Family and Child Therapist for more than fifteen years. Through therapy and seminars, Dr. Gruzen assists individuals and couples in creating better relationships with themselves and others. She conducts a private practice in Sherman Oaks, California, where she resides with her husband and two-year-old twin sons.

Rebecca Sperber holds a Master's Degree in Counseling and has been a licensed Marriage, Family and Child Therapist for twelve years. She specializes in working with individuals and couples on relationship enhancement and addiction recovery, with special emphasis on assertiveness training and improving self-esteem. She has written numerous articles about relationships and has appeared on talk shows throughout the country. The author is in private practice in Brentwood, California, where she resides with her husband and two young sons.

The authors would appreciate hearing stories from readers who benefit from this book or who are interested in receiving information about their seminars and other forthcoming publications.

Both authors are available for lectures and workshops based on this book. Details will be sent upon request.

They may be contacted as follows:

Phone: (310) 207-8552

E-mail: BetterDating@writeme.com

Address: Rebecca Sperber, M.S., M.F.C.C.
            12011 San Vicente Blvd., #305
            Los Angeles, CA 90049

or through their publisher:

Griffin Publishing Group
544 W. Colorado St.
Glendale, CA 91204-1102

Phone: (818) 244-1470

Fax: (818) 244-7408

E-mail: griffinbooks@earthlink.net

Website: www.griffinpublishing.com